Men of the Kingdom

Augustine: The Thinker

By

GEORGE W. OSMUN

WIPF & STOCK · Eugene, Oregon

Wipf and Stock Publishers
199 W 8th Ave, Suite 3
Eugene, OR 97401

Augustine
The Thinker
By Osmun, George W.
Softcover ISBN-13: 978-1-7252-8472-2
Hardcover ISBN-13: 978-1-7252-8474-6
eBook ISBN-13: 978-1-7252-8473-9
Publication date 7/15/2020
Previously published by Jennings and Graham, 1906

This edition is a scanned facsimile of the original
edition published in 1906.

TO
My Father and Mother

PREFACE

No ATTEMPT is made in this volume to glorify Augustine. The single aim is to present him as he was—to preserve him from his adulators. To omit the halo, is to be more just to him, and to be true to ourselves.

Augustine lived in an age which, though decadent, was tense with interest. Old institutions and religions were passing away. New races and a new religion were pressing forward for recognition and regnancy. Not least striking of the figures that move to and fro upon this kaleidoscopic panorama is that of the busy Bishop of Hippo. His own personal struggles and his contentions in behalf of the Faith are bound up with the great movements of his age. In several important senses he was a child of that age. But he nevertheless dominates it. And it is to his genius, largely, that Christianity owes its triumphant entry into the era which followed.

In fairness, therefore, both to Augustine and his age, I have tried to show how he and the forces of his time interacted upon one another.

In the performance of my task I have been under obligation to a great mass of literature bearing upon Augustine. Of this I would acknowledge especially Joseph McCabe's brilliant "Saint Augustine and His Age" (though I have found myself in constant dissent from his implications), and to Neander's discriminating and scholarly "History of the Christian Church." For unusual privileges and great courtesy I would also express my gratitude to the Rev. Samuel Ayres, B. D., librarian of the Drew Seminary.

WESTHAMPTON, L. I., April 17, 1906.

CONTENTS

CHAPTER		PAGE
I.	GETTING A START,	11
II.	CARTHAGE AND THE DAWN OF AN IDEAL,	21
III.	MANI,	30
IV.	THE IMPERIAL CITY,	44
V.	IN THE CITY OF AMBROSE,	55
VI.	THROUGH PLATO TO CHRIST,	67
VII.	CASSICIACUM,	81
VIII.	BACK TO AFRICA,	93
IX.	HIPPO REGIUS,	107
X.	THE BISHOP AT WORK,	121
XI.	DONATUS,	140
XII.	THE TWO CITIES,	161
XIII.	LABORS—LITERARY AND THEOLOGICAL,	183
XIV.	THE PELAGIANS,	201
XV.	AUGUSTINE AND THE FINAL STRUGGLE,	224
XVI.	THE STREAM OF AUGUSTINIANISM,	242

FIRST PERIOD

FROM NOVEMBER 13, 354 A. D. TO EASTER, 387 A. D.

CHAPTER I.

GETTING A START.

If you follow the southern coast-line of the Mediterranean east from the Pillars of Hercules, you come at length to a great promontory jutting into the sea toward the Island of Sicily. In the day of our story, this promontory was dominated by the presence of historic Carthage. But of deeper interest to us is a very much smaller town, Thagaste, that lay some twoscore miles to the south. For here at Thagaste, exactly five hundred years after the fall of the first Carthage, was born Aurelius Augustinus, familiar in history as St. Augustine, Bishop of Hippo.

Thagaste stood on the first of a series of broadly-sloping terraces, which, climbing up from the broken neck of Carthaginian territory, and reaching westward to the far-away white summits of the Atlas, formed the provinces of Numidia and Mauritania. Favored by a moderate climate, made fertile by abundant streams, sheltered by the overtowering mountain ranges, sweetened by the breath of the sea, it is not surprising that these swelling plateaus abounded in wealth, and were covered with hundreds of thriving towns and villages.

By the middle of the fourth century the Romanization of North Africa had been long since complete. Numidia was annexed to Rome under Julius Cæsar, while Claudius, about a century later, added Mauritania. Everywhere the organization and thrift of the empire were manifest. To lordly Roman families had been assigned the vast estates, whose waving fields of corn, tilled by native slaves, constituted the granary of the Mistress City, and brought an unprecedented prosperity and luxury. So there grew up numberless colonies, joined firmly by the world-famed imperial roads. Some of these towns reproduced the magnificence of Rome itself in walls and gates, mausoleums, amphitheaters, baths, basilicas, and temples, and arches of triumph. All this display was made possible by the iniquitous fiscal policy of Rome. But the taxes became so excessive as to impose an intolerable burden upon the shoulders of the middle classes, and this "Soul of the Empire" was gradually crushed till the day of the invading Vandal, who laid low the Roman rule and the Roman glory. However, until that day, which was delayed until Augustine had finished his labors, the mixed population of the towns gave themselves up to the glittering life which Augustine himself compared "to glass in its fragile splendor."[1]

The Christian Church had, indeed, followed close in the wake of the Roman seizure of North Africa. It was here that the first Latin

---
[1] City of God, IV, 3.

GETTING A START.

version of the Scriptures originated. A century and a half before our date, the first great Latin apologist, Tertullian, had hurled his defense of Christianity against the pagans. From him we learn that even so early the triumph of the Church had been far-reaching. "We leave you your temples only. We can count your armies. Our number in a single province will be greater."

It must be confessed, however, that the Christian ardor of the earlier days had grown measurably cooler in the presence of the pomp and worldliness of the times. There had been numerous lapses under the keen persecutions of Decius and Diocletian. But it is to be feared that the presence of material prosperity and prevailing corruption was much more effective in reducing the number of Christians. Even among those who were numbered as Christians, Christianity was in many cases hardly an affair of passion. The master-passion of those days was rather the games and public spectacles. If these chanced on the same day with the religious feasts or worship in the Churches, the latter generally proved the sufferers by being less popular. So much was this so that a convention at Carthage, in 401, appealed to the emperor to cause the transfer of the public shows from days distinctly Christian to other days of the week. Augustine himself complains,[2] on a certain day given to pagan festivals, of the slight attendance upon his preaching, of

---
[2] Tractate VII, 2, on the Gospel of St. John.

men, and especially of women, "whom, if not fear, modesty at all events ought to deter from the public scene."

Unfortunately the North African Church was weighted also with a persistent schism. It will fall to our lot later to consider the part Augustine took in what is known as the Donatist controversy. For now it is enough to record the fact that for many years already Donatism had been waging a relentless war on the Catholic Church. The emperor, Constantine, had found it impossible to stay the ravages of the schism by imperial edict, and now the entire Church of Africa was rent asunder by the obstinate disputes of the rival parties. In most of the towns was presented the unedifying spectacle of basilicas and bishops opposed to one another, heated public debates, services interrupted by fierce onslaughts, and even bloodshed and family strife—all in the name of religion.

The town of Thagaste doubtless reflected most of these ecclesiastical and political conditions at the time of Augustine's birth, November 13, 354. His mother was a Christian. Without attempting to glorify Monica, as many have done, we may accept Augustine's own estimate of her "devout conversation toward God" and "her holy tenderness and attentiveness" to her son.[3] It can hardly be doubted that Augustine owed a vast debt to his godly mother for her prayers and unconquerable

---
[3] Confessions, IX, 33.

Getting a Start.

love, as he received from her also that religious yearning, which did not forsake him even in his worst years. So much can not be spoken for the father. Patricius was an unlovely, poor freeman, with crude tastes and of a shallow, harsh disposition. A man requiring constant propitiation to prevent passionate outbursts of anger, with no principles to deter him from shameless disregard of his marriage vows, he would in our day be catalogued as a heartless brute. But even him Monica gained over to a Christian confession before his death. To them, in addition to Aurelius, were born a son, Navigius, and a daughter, both of whom were Christians.

At his birth, Augustine tells us, he was sprinkled with salt and signed with the cross, signifying his admission as a candidate for baptism. As to the various attitudes of his infancy, the presumed sins of little indignations and pale jealousies and bitter looks, of which we read in the Confessions, it is hardly proper to speak, since Augustine himself makes considerate avowal of his having received these details from another or "guessed them from other infants."

"After that I was put to school to get learning. And if slow to learn I was flogged."[4] The millennial period for boys, of abandoning corporeal inflictions, had not yet arrived, and Augustine seems to have had no exemption from a due share of "stripes." "One and one are two" was a "hateful

---

[4] Confessions, I, 14.

song" to him, ball-playing and shows offered more attractions than obedience to his teachers, while he chafed under the inconsistency of his elders, calling their idleness "business" and his games "trifling."

With all his early detestation of learning, Augustine soon showed himself to be a youth of rare memory and capacity. Reading, writing, and arithmetic gave way at length to the higher training under the "grammarian." With the increased dignity attaching to this salaried teacher, whose schoolroom was separated from the vestibule by an impressive curtain, and with far less prosaic studies to awaken his imagination, Augustine became a more devoted student. To what keen-fancied boy, reared within a day's journey of mighty Carthage, would not tales, in his native tongue, of the sack of Troy and the coming of Æneas, have abiding interest? The mythologies of Rome, too, and the wondrous deeds of the men of the empire, were surely to Augustine the lad more than the "pleasant spectacle of vanity" which they became to Augustine the mature ecclesiastic.

Toward the study of Greek, however, Augustine showed a positive aversion, probably because he was "compelled to learn" it. "The difficulty of learning a Greek language mingled with gall all the sweetness of those fabulous Grecian stories."[5] It is for this that Augustine preferred in later years the Latin version of Platonist writings,[6] and felt him-

---

[5] Confessions, I, 23.   [6] Confessions, VIII, 13.

self too little acquainted with the Greek tongue to read and understand therein discussions upon abstract themes.[7] But he seems, with advancing years, to have mastered his Greek sufficiently for appreciation of the Greek texts of Scripture.[8]

By the time Augustine was fourteen, he had fitted himself for studies still more advanced. Because of his uncommon ability, his parents determined he should receive advantages superior to those at Thagaste. Accordingly he was sent to Madaura for training in rhetoric. Already he had developed a fond hospitality to the follies of the merry world about him. And though he was "softened by friendship" and "shunned sorrow, meanness, and ignorance," he was not a stranger to lying, pilfering, deceit, and pride. During a sudden illness—probably nothing more serious than always happens to boys who are "enslaved by gluttony" and steal from their "parents' table and cellar"[9]—he wished vigorously for Christian baptism. This his pious mother was on the point of providing for, when he quickly recovered. Hence the rite was deferred, for in those days it was often customary to put off baptism till the close of life, as in the case of the Emperor Constantine. Thus it could be said, in accord with a wooden notion of this sacred sacrament: "Let him alone, let him act as he likes, for he is not yet baptized."[10]

---

[7] On the Trinity, III, 1.   [8] Cf. On Christian Doctrine, II, 11-15.
[9] Confessions, I, 30.   [10] Confessions, 1, 18.

At Madaura, twenty miles farther south in the Province of Numidia, the prevalent Roman influences and pagan practices were not calculated to advance Augustine in piety or to put a check upon his restless nature. The powers at Rome were just then more tolerant of the heathen cults, as was partly evident from the statues of the gods, reared everywhere in the town, and especially from the majestic image of Mars in the Forum. But these were only the bolder marks of the pagan atmosphere which pervaded the place. The majority of the populace were not in sympathy with the religion of his mother. And though he was still a catechumen, and perhaps quartered with Christian relatives, the magic enchantments of heathenism must have woven themselves about his eager mind. By a boy, who had already found the easy path of vice, there was little to be desired in the worship of the crude Christian chapel, as compared with the elaborate ritual of the temples. In later years, Augustine addressed the "men of Madaura" as "his fathers," but he could never tear from his mind the impressions made there by his witnessing the sacrilegious Bacchanalia.

His study of rhetoric hardly contributed to any lingering loyalty he may have had for the truth. The pursuit of the fine art of declamation, with minute attention to "inferences, definitions, and divisions,"[11] was meant primarily to produce mere

---

[11] On Christian Doctrine, II, 55. Cf. IV, 1-5.

cleverness in oratory. Learning was becoming more and more a thing of conventions. Depth and philosophic outlook were sacrificed to polish and sophistry. To be sure Augustine was intended for the bar, and to be a successful pleader in his day one must be ingeniously plausible. Hence the formal mastery of rhetorical devices was indispensable. Still one may be pardoned for wishing, after a prolonged exploration of many of Augustine's labyrinthine diffusions, that he had become possessed of the art of curtailment as well as that of elaboration. Certainly Augustine was not deepened by contact with the superficial studies and pagan masters of Madaura.

At any rate, this period of unrestrained familiarity with the ways of the world and of shallow learning, fitted Augustine for a perilous susceptibility to what awaited him during the year to follow at Thagaste. The ambition of Patricius for his son, led him to go beyond his means, in order to send Augustine away for a further residence at Carthage. But a year was needed for full arrangements, and this time Augustine spent in frivolity and idleness. He became involved in the wanton comradery of reckless fellows of the town, among whom he was "ashamed to be less shameless." The admonitions of his fearful mother he regarded only as "womanish counsels," which he would blush to obey.

Patricius was just winning the praise of his fellow-townsmen for the laudable sacrifices in behalf of his son, when his death seemed to bring Augustine's career to a sudden stop. The "Confessions" make only a passing notice of the demise of his father, so that there was doubtless no great friendship between them. Fortunately, at this crisis, a wealthy decurion Romanianus, whose generosity Augustine never forgot, received the promising lad into his house and provided funds for his advance along the highway of knowledge. Thus was Augustine's face turned towards Carthage and the long struggle for truth.

CHAPTER II.

CARTHAGE, AND THE DAWN OF AN IDEAL.

THE situation of ancient Carthage was too strategic for it to remain long unoccupied after its ruthless destruction by Africanus in 146 B. C. Many years had not passed before colonies set out from Rome to re-people and resurrect the City of Hannibal. These beginnings, under Gaius Gracchus and Julius Cæsar, came to higher completion when Augustus, a century after its ruin, made Carthage the proconsular seat of Africa. With this outward restoration of the former Punic glory, New Carthage became a center of Roman corruption and reckless living. Upon the abruptly rising citadel-hill called Byrsa, was reared in honor of the "deified man," Æsculapius, a new temple, approached by a wide terrace of sixty stairs. On the same summit, overlooking the two busy harbors, stood a beautiful palace of Rome's representative, at one time the historian Sallust. Once more the reservoirs on the south and west, and the huge aqueduct from the distant hills, poured their waters into the city below; outgoing ships bore their burdens of corn to Rome and the East, and returning, stuffed Carthage with wealth and luxury; in the broad Forum at the foot of the hill a transformed senate-house was alive with demagogues, and the Temple of Apollo with its worshipers; life in Carthago Nova became an alluring passion with the Roman aristocracy, and their sumptuous houses resounded with revelry and debauch.

It is doubtless true that Roman Carthage was religious. But religion included the worst abominations of paganism. The hideous cult of Saturn had been suppressed by a severe visitation upon its votaries. But a temple to the god had been built with great magnificence upon the ruins of the former temple to the same deity. For heathenism persisted in Carthage longer than in Rome. The Carthaginians still worshiped images of the old Tyrian Hercules. Once, when a magistrate ventured to order the head of Hercules to be gilded, Augustine tells us the Christian part of the populace were excited with such furious zeal, that special measures had to be taken by the bishops to prevent violence. Worst of all, if there could be a deeper depth, was the worship connected with the gigantic temple of the goddess Cœlestis,[1] with its two-mile inclosure. This temple, which, previous to its destruction, was looked upon as one of the architectural triumphs of the age, was restored by Augustus, and its shameless practices continued in Carthage long after Rome had ceased to counte-

---

[1] Greek Aphrodite, Latin Venus, Syrian Astarte.

nance them. Through the streets of the city wandered the strange creatures who passed as priests of this licentious cult. Augustine himself gives a gruesome picture of the ceremonies which were a daily occurrence before the shrine of this vulgar "virgin goddess." From all sides a vast crowd have gathered and stand closely packed together as they worship, "with prayer and with obscene rites." There are met immodest stage girls, women of base intent, foul-mouthed men, profligates, and harlots, who glory in the sight, that greets their eyes, of nameless vices, enacted by lewd prayers, with a pretense of reverence.[2]

If Carthage was religious, it was even more persistently bent on pleasure. Following the fashion set by Rome, with her Circus Maximus, the Carthaginians became as intense devotees of the Circensian pastimes as they were of the temples. Augustine seems not to have shared in this fondness for the circus, nor for the ruder debauch of the gladiatorial combats. Before many years he counted it a joy to have rescued a young friend from their fascination. But he became familiar with them, and in later days acknowledged how slight were the attractions of Christian worship and preaching when the exhibitions were in progress.

It was the theater which especially attracted Augustine. What appealed to him there was the vivid representation of such human follies and

---
[2] City of God, II, 26.

weaknesses as were beginning to get a firm grip upon his own life.[3] It was not surprising that the early Church adopted such stern measures against the stage-plays, and excluded from baptism those who attended them. Whatever may have been the quality of the stage in the earlier history of the empire, it is certain that it had touched its lowest depths by the time Augustine went as a student to Carthage. Not only were actors cut off from all civic honors, and actresses looked upon as infamous —the drama itself had become mere dribble and obscenity. Legerdemain, crude pantomime, and coarse jesting supplied surfeit to the sordid appetites of the populace. Mr. McCabe finds Augustine's conduct in youth "unusually regular," and hardly takes the "Confessions" seriously. He cites the testimony of Vincentius, a Rogatian bishop, to the effect that when they were acquaintances in Carthage, Augustine was "a quiet and respectable youth,"—but he neglects Augustine's reply that "not every one who is indulgent is a friend" and "you know me now to be more desirous of rest, and earnest in seeking it, than when you knew me in my earlier years in Carthage." At any rate, Augustine's patronage of these degrading "exhibitions of stupid buffoonery" is evidence enough of a lamentable morbidness and grossness of taste.

Any lingering indisposition to admit this ought to be overborne by certain other considerations. In

---
[3] Confessions, III, 3.

The Dawn of an Ideal. 25

addition to the morally tainted atmosphere he was breathing in the temples, the games, and the theatricals, Augustine was occupying only a shallow relation to the Church. Though he continued to attend Christian services, he had no other than a conventional motive for doing so. He was a catechumen still, and Christianity was the confession of his mother; therefore, he went into the basilicas with other catechumens. But his meditations there were anything but devout—indeed, were wandering constantly to forbidden objects of sinful desire.[4] It may be he found little encouragement in the Church. The influence of Cyprian still hung as a kind of halo over the city. But it was not an age remarkable for piety. Accessions in large numbers were not wanting. But conversions which signified, as Neander puts it, "an exchange of open, undisguised paganism, for a nominal Christianity covering a pagan way of thinking," far exceeded in number the conversions which reached and transformed the inner disposition. Augustine complains that the Church is full of the former kind, and "seldom is Jesus sought for Jesus' sake."[5] Immorality, drunkenness, and rioting were common among members of the Church. And in these respects the young student must have found slight distinction between Christian and pagan. But it doubtless caused him little concern.

The fact is, his studies at this time were not

---

[4] Confessions, III, 5.   [5] On the Gospel of John, Tractate, 20, 10.

leading in the direction of lofty thought. At the university he made rapid advance. But he admits that craftiness was the mark of attainment. The lack of moral earnestness apparent in the living of the men of his day showed itself also in their culture. Rhetorical flourish and embellished phrase were made a deceptive garb for such scraps of Greek philosophy as could be combined into an artificial "system," which in reality was only a "literary medley." Grammar and rhetoric were the chief departments of study, and we must not, of course, underestimate the great proficiency which was attained by such men as Augustine in dialectics and the principles of eloquent discourse, nor the vast amount of information which they had ready at their command. In addition to rhetoric, logic, music, arithmetic, and geometry constituted the daily round of Augustine's intellectual pursuit. Besides this, as a task outside the regular curriculum, he mastered Aristotle's "ten categories." On the other hand, any one at all acquainted with the works of Augustine must have noticed the hollowness of a great deal of his reasoning. Under conditions, in which casuistry and declamation were made easy substitutes for profound thinking, one can hardly expect to find a youth progressing fast in the art of high living.

Conditions were hardly improved for Augustine by his associates. To put it mildly, they were bent on mischief rather than learning. They were under no restraint of discipline, would burst in upon

The Dawn of an Ideal.

a master with wild gesticulations and impudent indignities, and upon the street greeted strangers with jeers and unpardonable insolence.[6] It is true Augustine reprobated the worst of their crude revelry. Nevertheless he rather shamefacedly admits he "was delighted with their friendship at times."

During this period also Augustine formed the illicit alliance which embittered his entire after life. Nothing can be gained by attempting to smooth over this transaction. As has been shown repeatedly, he felt the Christian standard of living which his mother exemplified. It was this standard, and not the weak substitutes for it which, in the world around him, glared defiance to known moral demands, that made Augustine conscious also of living below his own ideal. His sin looks no less ugly because of its setting in an age which was tolerant of profligacy. As to the character and social rank of Augustine's mistress, there can be little profit in making inquiry, especially as the "Confessions" reveal so little. To her, at least, it is creditable that for fourteen years they lived in mutual fidelity —a fact remarkable in a day of disgusting moral laxity—and that upon her release she seems to have entered upon a life of purity. Augustine, according to the highest ethical principles, should have married her instead of casting her off only to take up with another. But the "Confessions" must be accepted at their face-value. In them, the sorrowing

---

[6] Confessions, III, 6, and V, 14.

bishop laid bare to mankind the pitiful truth, and mankind must judge in mercy. With all that may be searched out to disintensify the blackness of the youth's sad plight, it was too black, a thing to regret, both for what it was, and for what it uncovered of inward foulness. But no regret for it could be keener than Augustine's own.

We are therefore compelled to believe that Augustine's experience was as bad as he makes it out. The conflict had begun in him of the young man whose vision has far outrun his grasp. But he had not forsaken all his best. For one thing a proud ambition stirred in his breast. He had made some attainment, and was conscious of superiority over his fellows. An eagerness for knowledge took hold of him. Possibilities of honorable distinction beckoned him on to the heights. Perhaps already he was casting about for a safe path out of the moral wilderness into which he was plunged. It was in a mood like this that he happened upon a treatise of Cicero, the "Hortensius," now unfortunately lost. The importance of this book at such a crisis can be estimated from its effect upon the young rhetorician. In face of its exhortation to philosophy, erudition and decorations of style became of minor importance. "Worthless suddenly became every vain ambition to me; and, with an incredible warmth of heart, I yearned for an immortality of wisdom, and began now to arise that I might return unto Thee." Whatever had been his dream of wealth, rank, and worldly happiness, this work set his dream at rest. Here, then, was a new and splendid inspiration. It had in it no reformatory power. But it enlisted Augustine in the long quest of wisdom. God had hung in the skies an ideal.

CHAPTER III.

MANI.

When Augustine declares[1] that the ardor newly awakened by the "Hortensius" did not take complete hold of him, because he failed to find in the book the name of Christ, he is not to be taken too literally.[2] What he doubtless means is, that from a Christian point of view there was no moral settlement for him except in Christ. The man who opens his "Confessions" with the familiar words: "Thou hast formed us for Thyself, and our hearts are restless till they find rest in Thee," is the man who has experienced the absoluteness of the Christian faith. No message of a pagan philosopher, however high-minded, could speak a final word to him.

But the "Hortensius" did give a directive word, and Augustine followed it. In this way he fell to reading the Scriptures. If it is true that he read the earliest Latin translation, which had been used in Africa from the days of Tertullian, we can understand somewhat the repulsion he felt at its rude, even barbarous style, "unworthy to be compared with the dignity of Tully."[3] To a proud young

---

[1] Confessions, III, 8.
[2] Cf., e. g., McCabe, St. Augustine and His Age, p. 54.
[3] Confessions, III, 9.

student with whom ornate phraseology was a first requisite of culture, the inartistic African version was ugly, indeed, even repulsive. And there was a second reason. All athirst as he was for wisdom, he could hardly be expected to endure the intolerance of an apostle who threw to the winds the "wisdom" of the Greeks, and preached a doctrine of "foolishness." Presumably there were still other burdens connected with his acceptance of the Old Testament, for even among Christians of the West there was a widely sown distaste for that part of the Scriptures. In this condition of mind, Augustine was quite susceptible to any philosophy, even the shallowest, which made a show of religion, and was prepared to answer his questions. Because it seemed to fit into this dire situation, he turned now to the system known as Manichæism.

According to the Arabic tradition, Mani, the founder of the system, was a Persian of high birth, who, in answer to angelic visitations, separated himself from the Parsism of his father about 238 A. D. Claiming to be the Paraclete promised by Jesus, and deriving his teachings from the Magi and the Christians, he journeyed in many lands for forty years, scattering his doctrines in India, China, and Turkestan. Eventually he returned to Persia, gained favor in the court, but at length was crucified by order of King Bahraim I (about 276), and his skin, stuffed with straw, was hung at the city gate. Meanwhile his twelve apostles had spread

Westward and had won many disciples. According to one account a special envoy was sent to Africa by Mani himself. There, in spite of the rigorous edicts of Diocletian, Valentinian and Theodosius, the sect made continued progress down to Augustine's time.

But what was there in Mani which fascinated Augustine and held him more or less closely captive for nine years? The religion of Mani in the West took far more account of historical Christianity than did Mani himself. It grounded itself upon a conception of Deity which was meant to solve the world-old problems of the existence of evil. There were two eternal beings—one, the King of the Paradise of Light; the other, Darkness. These two kingdoms border upon one another, but during the uncounted ages before creation exist in separation. Now begins the enactment of a vast tragedy. Forth from the Kingdom of Darkness proceeds Satan bent upon destruction; he is met by the armed Knight of Light who suffers defeat. Whereupon Satan snatches away and imprisons elements of the Spiritual Kingdom. Out of the commingling of elements is born the world. Here the unceasing contest is prolonged, the sun meantime receiving whatever liberated light has been mingled with "hot devils," and the moon, that mingled with "cold devils," while man is a child of demons in whom are concentrated and locked up the captive elements of light. But a fatal entanglement of these, with sensuality and covetousness, makes for man a dual soul, one of good, and one of evil. Life becomes what we actually see it to be in the world—a struggle between the principles of good and evil.

But what hope did Mani give that men might eventually escape from the Kingdom of Darkness and find refuge in the Kingdom of Light? It is here more especially that the Manichæans of the West departed widely from the teaching of Mani. To him Jesus was merely a Jewish abomination. Although Augustine says that he styled himself "Manichæus, an Apostle of Jesus Christ," it is certain that he regarded Christ not as real, but as a spiritual fancy. As for salvation, there was none possible except through ceremonial observances and a life severely ascetic. But as Manichæism came into contact with Christianity, it took to itself much of the outward aspect of the latter. A pretended acceptance of the New Testament, a certain loyalty to Christ, a pronounced emphasis on the doctrine of Redemption, a call for earnest self-denial—such notes in their appeal to Western Christians made it possible for the Manichæans to gain many proselytes. But Manichæism was far from being, as it is often represented,[4] "practically a Christian heresy." Its resemblance to Christianity, so far as can be seen, was purely superficial. In one respect, it openly antagonized Christianity—it utterly cast

---

[4] Cf. Rainy, The Ancient Catholic Church, p. 267.

off the Old Testament. Perhaps this was one of the chief features which commended the system of Mani to seekers like Augustine. As already noticed, the Old Testament Scriptures were passing through the fires, much as in our day. And Christian teachers, like Augustine later, and like many "trembling evangelicals," as Professor Rendel Harris has called them, of a still later era, were doing little to meet the attacks made upon the morality and religious teaching of the Old Testament. Instead of argument and manly courage they presented forced allegorical interpretations which only made the difficulties bigger.[5]

Another element in Manichæism, which proved attractive, was its system of morals. Among its elect, there was expected thorough separation from everything sordid and sensual—animal food, wine, and "worldly" interests. In addition, chastity, rigorous fastings, systematic prayer, and sacred ablutions were enjoined. A lower order of discipleship was recognized, the *auditores,* but much greater laxity was permitted them. Augustine never advanced beyond the position of a "hearer," and upon his complete release did not hesitate to bring heavy charges against the elect. Whether these aspersions were well founded or not is not clear. Some Manichæans evidently practiced and could be detected by a certain gauntness and pallor of countenance. It is even said that "Manichæan" became a

---

[5] Cf. Kingsley's truthful representation in Hypatia, Chap. XXI.

by-word for any one who "did not appreciate the felicity of good living."[6] But it is evident that the morality of the Manichæans was heathen rather than Christian, and that the profession was rarely borne out in practice. The extreme doctrinaire Manichæans of Augustine's day formed themselves into a distinct sect at Rome, under the leadership of a wealthy zealot, Constantius by name. But most of them found the discipline too harsh, and, following the example of Faustus, forsook the habit of sleeping on mats (whence they were known as Mattarians), and slunk quietly away to their feathers and goatskin coverlets. So we find Augustine making a fling at the arrogance of Faustus, the keenest and most unscrupulous enemy of Christianity in his age.[7] Nevertheless, it is not difficult to see how enticing such pretensions, especially when made with earnestness, would be in an age in which pagan ascetic notions had already crept into the Church.

There is, however, reason for believing that the fundamental explanation of the rapid spread of Manichæism is, as Professor Harnack has shown,[8] that it was the most artistic and richest philosophic attempt to disentangle the knotty problems of the origin and meaning of evil. It brought down to a tangible plain the mysteries of moral darkness and

---

[6] Cf. Jerome, De Custod. Virg., Ep. 18: "Quam viderint pallentem atque tristem, Miseram, Monacham, et Manichæam vocant."

[7] Reply to Faustus, The Manichæan, v. 7.

[8] Article, Manichæism, Encyclopædia Britannica.

light. By its fantastic parables of the struggles of the human soul it caught and held the attention of many disturbed minds. Then—a factor which probably drew Augustine into its fold—it held forth the possibility of a gradual unfolding of a secret wisdom, and the final disappearance of all barriers to the truth.

Whatever may have been the motive that led Augustine to cast his lot with the Manichæans, or the fervor of his first devotion to the new sect, it can hardly be thought that his eyes remained long unopened, or that his attachment was ever very real. It is far more probable that, for the next decade, he was casting about helplessly in a restless confusion of unstable ideas, trying to persuade himself that the light had dawned upon him, but unable to escape the insistent voice of his own conscience. True it is that he displayed surprising gullibility in crediting such absurd vagaries as that a fig-tree wept when plucked, and its fruit, eaten by a Manichæan "saint," forthwith exhaled particles of God and of angels.[9] Doubtless, also, Augustine proved a successful proselyter and induced many of his friends to join the Manichæans. Little wonder that the pious Monica was shocked beyond measure by the change which had come over her son, or that, grieved by such blasphemies as his derision of sacred things, she refused him shelter in her house. For in his twentieth year Augustine

---

[9] Cf. Confessions, III, 18; and Against Faustus, XXXI, 5.

had completed his course at Carthage and had returned to the home of his boyhood. His mother speedily found solace for her sorrow. First by a dream, in which Augustine appeared with her on a symbolic wooden rule, she became convinced he would some day embrace her faith. This new hope was strengthened by the famous conference with a certain ecclesiastic, who, though he saw how intractable and proud-spirited the young Augustine was, could not answer the argument of her importunate tears. "Go thy way," he said, "and God bless thee, for it is not possible that the son of these tears should perish." This she accepted as a voice from heaven.

At Thagaste, Augustine set up a school for instruction in rhetoric or grammar, possibly both. In this occupation, "amid much smoke," he sent forth "some flashes of fidelity."[10] By smoke he probably means his confessed passionate self-indulgence, his continued fondness for public spectacles, and his wallowing in Manichæan mire. But there were also "flashes of fidelity." With great diligence he devoted himself to his studies. In these he was to find his surest way out of the delusions into which he had fallen. A mind which reveled in the rugged matter-of-fact philosophy of Aristotle could not long remain unconscious of the ludicrous nature of the Manichæan error. But it is a characteristic of Augustine's mental unsettlement dur-

---

[10] Confessions, IV, 2.

ing this time, that, along with his philosophical researches, he mingled enough zeal for the weird Manichæan speculations to make him earnest in his efforts to secure converts.[11]

Thus, teaching, studying, proselyting, he continued a year or so in his native town Thagaste. Among his pupils were the two sons of his wealthy patron, Romanianus, and Alypius, who belonged to an honorable family and was marked out for a distinguished career. Of still another friend, Augustine speaks in terms which reveal an uncommon affection. This youth had shared with him the frolics and studies of the earlier years in Thagaste, and had turned Manichæan under Augustine's leadership. The two now became inseparable, "Nor could my soul exist without him." But ere a year had passed of this renewed friendship—"sweet to me above all the sweetness of my life"—a fever laid the young man low. None but Augustine's own words, written years afterwards, can properly convey his feelings: "At this sorrow my heart was utterly darkened, and whatever I looked upon was death. My native country was a torture to me, and my father's house a wondrous unhappiness; and whatsoever I had participated in with him, wanting him, turned into a frightful torture. Mine eyes sought him everywhere, but he was not granted them; and I hated all places because he was not in them; nor could they now say to me, 'Behold, he

---

[11] On Two Souls, Against the Manichees, IX.

is coming,' as they did when he was alive and absent. I became a great puzzle to myself, and asked my soul why she was so sad, and why she so exceedingly disquieted me; but she knew not what to answer me. So I fretted, sighed, wept, tormented myself, and took neither rest nor advice." It is in such human passages as this that one finds what was Augustine's nature at bottom—the abode of warm affections and quick sympathies. If the sterner features of the grim fighter are more noticeable in the later years, it is not because human tenderness was crushed out (for one discovers gleams of it in many of the letters to the last), but because the busy bishop of Hippo became so entirely absorbed in the contests which were fought out over his deepest convictions.

Although in addressing himself to Romanianus,[12] Augustine seems to indicate a lower motive—namely, to find a higher position—we may credit his statement that his real reason, for now turning his face toward Carthage again, was a desire to get away from the scenes of his shattered friendship. Hither some of his pupils repaired with him to enter his school of rhetoric. A talented lad, Nebridius by name, and another called Eulogius, were added to the number. Alypius also went to Carthage, but did not at first attend the school owing to an ill-feeling which had arisen between his father and Augustine. Though a youth

---

[12] Against the Academics.

of singular virtue, Alypius soon fell into the entangling habits of the gayer set of Carthage, especially of those who followed the Circensian games. Augustine knew his promise and longed to rescue him. But no way appeared until one day the lad chanced to saunter into the lecture-room, contrary to his father's command, and the rhetoric-master, wishing to make plain a matter in hand, resorted to a figure drawn from the circus, seizing the opportunity thus presented to expose the madness of those who frequented the games. Though unintentionally, this reference proved a God-send to Alypius, who from that day abandoned the pastimes and became a regular pupil.[13]

One of the pastimes of Carthage was the fine art of divination. In after years Augustine describes the votaries of astrologers as "deluded and imposed upon by the false angels." But he himself appears to have been a willing votary during his stay in Carthage, and indeed for several years after. We may give him credit for frowning upon the more brutal practices of the soothsayers. There is an interesting account of one of these. Augustine was quite ambitious for success in the oratorical contests of the theaters. Upon one such occasion, he was approached by a magician who offered to slay certain creatures as sacrifices and to deliver to Augustine the coveted victory. But the answer came back sharply: "If the garland were of im-

---

[13] Cf. Confessions, VI, 11 and 12.

perishable gold, I would not suffer a fly to be destroyed to secure it for me." But the arts of the mathematicians which he came to look upon as a "baleful fellowship between man and devils," he now estimated of high value. In this he was not alone. Not only among the pagans, but even in the Church, were multitudes who staked everything upon the fictions of horoscope-casters.[14] What attracted Augustine was the large number of cases in which the truth was apparently foretold. The derisions of his young friend Nebridius did not suffice to dislodge him from his belief. An able physician, who was proconsul, Vindicianus, also undertook to dissuade him. But it was not until years after when Augustine was farther advanced in scientific study, and saw many pronounced failures to forecast the future, that he yielded and became as firm an opponent of all sorcery as he had been a sympathizer.

Doubtless Augustine's interest in divination was a part of his profounder study of astronomy. Through the latter he now came to perceive the unscientific character of the Manichæan teaching. He determined to probe into their books, and soon discovered many glaring discrepancies between their astronomic notions and the calculations of secular philosophers. A sect which taught that the waxing and waning of the moon was caused by receiving souls from matter as it were into a ship and trans-

---

[14] Confessions, VI, 8.

ferring them "into the sun as into another ship,"[15] and which maintained that the sun's light shone through a triangular aperture in the heavens,[16] was bound to lose cast with a young astrologer who was beginning to learn the truth. Matters came to a head with the visit to Carthage, in 383, of Faustus, Manichæan Bishop of Mileve. Augustine was then in his twenty-ninth year. He had eagerly desired a conversation with this Faustus, on account of his high reputation for learning, and his heralded ability to clear up all difficulties. He was found to be a man of deference and volubility. But his suave manners and fluent speech did not deceive the skilled rhetorician. Augustine quickly unmasked his lack of erudition. He wanted real answers to real problems, and he was not long in seeing that the far-famed Faustus was not the man to lighten him of his burdens. The one thing which elevated the Manichæan bishop in Augustine's eyes was his sincerity and modesty—he acknowledged his ignorance and refused to argue beyond his depths. Accordingly he set himself to certain literary pursuits with the rhetoric master, with a hope that they both might find more ground for their faith. But this arrangement was soon broken up. Faustus, we shall meet again, and shall find him something more than a clever talker—one of the most acute and witty debaters Augustine ever had to face.

---

[15] Cf. Ep. 55, 6.   [16] Reply to Faustus, XX, 6.

For Augustine the next step seemed to be in the direction of Rome. For one thing his friends had been holding out alluring inducements—there was greater opportunity for honor in "the Eternal City," and other temporal advantages of no mean character. These Augustine confesses were considerations with him. But he was already enjoying a comfortable living, and he had given up the pursuit of wealth. The thing which influenced him most was the prospect of greater quiet. At Carthage he was compelled to submit to the boisterous misbehavior of the students until it became an intolerable burden to the flesh. Without making an open break with the Manichees, therefore, he determined to take his leave of Africa. After nine years the veil was lifting. He was not free. Beyond, there appeared—nothing. But he resolved to fight his way through, trusting meanwhile to the eclectic philosophy of Cicero.

CHAPTER IV.

THE IMPERIAL CITY.

Monica was much disturbed by her son's determination to sail for Italy. She pleaded with him to remain, and when that was found to be of no avail, begged to accompany him. Augustine's response was not to his credit. Pretending that a delay was necessary for a favorable wind, he persuaded his mother to spend the night in a near-by chapel built in memory of Cyprian. That night his ship spread sail for Ostia. It is not evident what was Augustine's motive for this cowardly departure, but his later condemnation of the act[1] makes it certain that the motive was worthless.

Augustine's sojourn in Rome was not a long one. Moreover his opportunities for becoming acquainted with the great city were curtailed by a serious fever, and by his devotion to his studies and teaching. It is not very surprising, therefore, that he is comparatively silent as to the impressions made upon him by the life about him. But we can be in little doubt as to what those impressions were. In the unsparing scorn and intense disgust with which he describes the folly and degradation of the

---
[1] Confessions, V, 15.

imperial city through most of her history, we can discern the things which took hold of him most during the six months or so that he lived there.

The "glory" of Rome had not yet departed nor the gold become dim. There was the same restless, pleasure-seeking, unthinking life as in the golden days of Augustus. The crowds still surged from marble-colonnaded forum and "Sacred Way," to Jupiter's temple or the baths, or the vast circus. In capitol, mansion of the rich, coliseum, temple, wine-shop, no outlay was too great which would minister to a morbid desire for sensuous delight. Gluttony of the most repulsive type; disgusting display by both patrician devotee of Cybele and the no less luxuriously adorned follower of Christ; gladiatorial shows; shiftlessness and unrestraint among the young men (a "quarter of a million of stout frames rotting in idleness"); stupid debauch among the elders; bedizenment and moral darkness among the matrons—these mingled with the rush of gilded chariots, the splendor of the shops, the flash of gold and silks, the drunken revel, the frenzied dance, the hideous religious festivals, to give Rome her "glory"—and to make a fatter feast for the Vandal Vulture.

It is taking only a shallow view of all this to say that the fall of Rome is traceable to other causes than her vice. One finds no difficulty in massing together many economic and political reasons why the fall of the empire was hastened. It is true that incessant war, the splitting of East from West, the costly use of foreign military service, the growth of slavery and the degradation of the masses, the failure of the old religions, the poisonous, ruinous greed of emperors and senators, were responsible for an inner decay which made the outward overthrow a child's romp for the disciplined Germanic tribes. But what was at the root of all this demoralization? What save moral failure and an insidious corruption which ate out both physical vigor, and judgment, and patriotic concern? There was no forlorn policy, no shifting, uncertain, coward spirit of the empire under Gratian, Valentinian and Honorius, which did not grow naturally out of the soil in which they were fostered. Voluptuousness and vanity gave birth to national effeminacy, and this to indifference. Immersed in her monstrous vices, Rome actually ignored the crowding barbarians. She established the bounds of Roman dominion at the Rhine and Danube, and before she was aware, was on the defensive—and helpless.

Still, Rome was far from being irreligious. When Augustine came to the city, nominally if not enthusiastically a Manichæan, he fell in easily with that sect. From the famous description given by Jerome, in the very year Augustine was in Rome, it has been conjectured that the Manichæan women at least were true to their ascetic ideal. But this does not tally well with statements made by Augustine,

THE IMPERIAL CITY.   47

who, though he found refuge with a follower of Mani during his idleness, has no good word to speak either of their "driveling," "raving" philosophy, or of their "senseless and seducing continency."[2] In addition there was at Rome a wide-spread interest in the cults of the East, including a formidable following of the Persian Mithra, who was the supreme god of the Emperor Julian. Of intensely deeper interest was the struggle which Paganism was making to maintain its hold upon the popular mind. It is evident that the old worship was by no means dead. From scores of statues and images, the gods and goddesses still kept up their reign, while the father of them all, from the proud Capitoline, enthroned himself in gold and marble. Though we are assured that "a cloud of little gods, like so many flies,"[3] had long since deserted the altars of the city, there remained enough to satisfy the hearts of the most devout. These remaining divinities were at least determined there should be no failure in the corn crop. Seia was set to watch over its upspringing, Segetia, over its maturing, Tutilina, over its storage. And this was not enough: Proserpina must see that the corn germinated properly; while Nodotus, Volutina, Potelana, Hostilina, Flora, Lacturnus, Matuta, Runcina, and others unrecounted ("for," says Augustine, "I am sick of all this,"[4]) were intrusted with various important duties. Even

---

[2] Confessions, VI, 12.   [3] City of God, II, 22.
[4] City of God, IV, 8.

then there was necessity for deities in sickening numbers to be present at every movement of a man from the hour of his birth. Most unseemly of all were the coarse immoralities connected with the worship of these divinities. The nameless rites of Liber, described by Varro, happily had disappeared. But Berecynthia and her shameful ceremonies still fouled the city. Augustine makes horrified reference to what he himself witnessed. Rome was religious enough, but for the most part her religion was like her life—it had no moral bottom.

Christianity, however, had come to hold the balance of power. Beginning with Constantine, pagan practices were out of favor with nearly all the emperors. Constantine in 346, 353, and 356, had directed drastic measures against sacrifices and the worship of heathen images, had ordered all the temples closed, besides demolishing and plundering some of them, and had carried on relentless war in behalf of the final extirpation of paganism. A policy quite the reverse was pursued by Julian during his brief reign of twenty months, ending in June, 363. By adroit jugglery, by double-dealing, by cunning use of power, by surrounding himself with an atmosphere of intellectual and moral culture, Julian succeeded in reviving the worship of the sanctuaries, and in gaining many proselytes to paganism. The character of this dangerous foe of Christianity shows itself conspicuously in his behavior toward Athanasius, Bishop of Alexandria, in banishing whom he professed publicly: "It was a dangerous thing for so cunning and restless a man to be at the head of the people." But, in another letter to the Egyptian prefect, he laid bare the real reason—this Athanasius was bringing despite upon all the gods, and, godless wretch that he was, had dared to baptize noble Grecian women in the reign of Julian! At any rate, the heathen party had won a passing victory. Had the life of the emperor not been brought to a sudden close, during a campaign in Persia, doubtless Christianity would have suffered still more at his hands. As it was, the hopes of the gods were dashed to the ground, for Jovian and Valentinian, though tolerant of all creeds, were zealous Christians.

It was in the reign of Gratian (375-384) that paganism received a check which marked the beginning of its final collapse. Gratian considered the acceptance of the pontifical robe a manifest inconsistency in a Christian. He went eyer farther in ardent support of his faith. Two years before Augustine came to Rome (382) he turned into his treasury the estates of the temples. He sadly abridged the rights of priests and Vestals. Most intolerant of all in the eyes of the suffering pagan, he bore away the statue consecrated to Victory. Before this shrine the old pagan senators were wont to take their oaths of allegiance, to scatter incense, and to make fitting oblation to the goddess who was thought to have guided the empire through many perils. It was the one symbol in all the city that Roman senators might still worship as did their fathers before them. But Gratian's suppression of Victory was not to pass without a protest.[5] The pagan appeal to the emperor was voiced by one of the finer-fibered men of his time, Quintus Aurelius Symmachus, who, along with his participation in the more daring extravagances of the day—for he is credited with spending over four hundred thousand dollars in producing a single public spectacle—was deeply devoted to his religion, and is otherwise worthy of respect. But Gratian had no ear for the remonstrants. His policy was largely dictated by the Christian party, who at this juncture put a counter-petition in the hands of Ambrose, the Bishop of Milan, where the father of Gratian had set up his court. The Roman Bishop Damasus added whatever further weight was needed, and there was no alternative for the youthful emperor. His indolent reign was cut short by his murder, at the hands of his own cavalry, the very next year, 383. The second Valentinian was only thirteen years of age when he succeeded his brother, and the pagan party saw an immediate opportunity. Several members of the privy council of the emperor were pagans. With him the political situation would doubtless count for more than the religious. Accordingly, in the year of Augus-

---

[5] Augustine says distinctly that a few years later "almost all the nobility of Rome were wedded to sacrilegious rites." (Confessions, VIII, 3.) But Ambrose and his followers maintained that the Christian element formed the major part of the senate.

tine's residence at Rome, the Prefect Symmachus again voiced a popular desire for the restoration of the statue of Victory. The privy council wavered, and Symmachus all but prevailed. Probably he would have done so had not Ambrose once more interfered. His letter to Valentinian, representing as it did the unyielding position of the Church, and tearing in shreds the casuistries of Symmachus, proved unanswerable. "If some nominal Christians advise you to such a course," he warns the boy-ruler, "do not be deceived by mere names. We bishops could not tolerate this. You might come to the church, but you would find your approach forbidden." The doughty Symmachus made two more efforts in the same direction, and was once rewarded for his persistency by banishment. But he was opposing an ever-increasing force. The old religion was crumbling into a hopeless ruin, while a new wonder was growing up by its side, a mountain that should fill the earth.

It is not to be thought, however, that the Christianity which Augustine found at Rome was above reproach. His own reasons for not being attracted to the Church were, first, that he kept up an external attachment to the Manichæans as a kind of temporary expedient. But the fact is, there was much that was hollow in the pretensions of the Church. It had all but given itself over to the entire reckless, self-indulgent spirit of the age. True, many aspects of Roman life have a brighter hue under the glow of Christian sentiment. Woman was beginning to enter upon a new inheritance of freedom, and divorce was under improved legal restrictions. Slavery was still prevalent, and the slave-trade flourished; "cheap as a Sardinian" became a proverb. But much of the cruelty practiced upon the slaves had ceased, while on certain festivals, great liberties were allowed them. New moral demands were staring men everywhere in the face, as a result of the insistent presence in society of Christian ideals. Cultured pagans like Symmachus, Prætextatus, and the rhetorician Libanius found themselves shamed up to new heights of living. On the other hand, the Church was beginning to taste some of the inevitable fruits of its alliance with the State. And the fruits were bitter. When Constantine accepted the sign of the cross, and Christianity became the rule of the empire, it seemed like a priceless advantage compared with the stern rigor of recent persecutions. Cessation of the old conflict, in behalf of Christ, through the disarming of foes, the approval of society, the widening of doors of service by imperial favor, revenues, immunities—this was surely a most captivating prospect. So were fostered secularity, greed, pride, hypocrisy, and many another evil. Membership in the Church became easy. Worldly corruption stalked into the holy of holies, and maintained its place under cover of the organization. When the pagans complained that enormous vice was supported beneath the show

THE IMPERIAL CITY. 53

of Christianity, and that the spread of Christianity was due largely to the favor of princes, Church apologists at least could not deny the facts.[6] Even among the clergy, moral laxity, worldly-mindedness, and ignorance were shamefully common. In a keenly sarcastic letter to the nun Eustochium, Jerome exposed, to the discomfiture of the Church, many of the more brazen faults of the Roman priesthood. Other letters of his constitute sad features of the picture.[7]

There is more than passing interest in this presence of Jerome in the Roman capital. Under the guidance of the grammarian Donatus he had received his early education there. Later he sought a desert seclusion in Syria, and, becoming a presbyter in Antioch, made his way to Rome in 382, on a visit to Damasus. At once Jerome sought to promote his monastic principles among people, most of whom were caught in the swirl of gayety about them. He preached his ascetic ideals to maidens and matrons of the first families of Rome. By his ardor and own rigid morality he induced many to abandon their homes and business, and in some instances to withdraw to the solitudes of Palestine. In all this, though he incurred displeasure on every side, he had the powerful support of his friend, the Bishop Damasus. But it so chanced that, in that eventful year 384, Damasus died, and was suc-

---

[6] Cf. e. g., Augustine, Sermon XV, and Ep. 136.

[7] Cf. Eps. 52, 24, 145, and 125.

ceeded by Siricius, a man who regarded Jerome's earnest effort to win Rome back to truth and righteousness as too radical. Accordingly, the learned monk shook from his feet the dust of the wicked Babylon.

It was at precisely the same time that the rhetoric-master, Augustine, for far different reasons, was also preparing to leave the great capital. As his instructions had been carried on at his own home, he had not shared in the munificent provision made for professors of rhetoric in his day. Hence he was in no financial position to endure the burden imposed by some of his tricky pupils. These young men were better behaved than those in Carthage, but they had one very serious defect. When payday came round they conspired to discredit their debt and to leave their master for another.[8] Most opportune, therefore, appeared a call from Milan for a public teacher of rhetoric. Before the prefect Symmachus, Augustine was found worthy of the appointment, which he received at once. He turned his back upon "Manichæan vanities," and at the public expense, made his journey along the Flaminian way to the city of Ambrose. Thus this polished Symmachus, in the very hour when he was contriving for the restoration of an expiring worship, was unwittingly contributing a new element of strength to the cause of his opponents.

---

[8] Confessions, V, 22.

CHAPTER V.

IN THE CITY OF AMBROSE.

AUGUSTINE was not to be alone in his new labors as professor at the University of Milan. A little circle of friends quickly closed around him, to share the trials of what was to prove one of the most burdensome, as well as momentous, periods of his life. Grave business matters had brought his steadfast benefactor Romanianus to the city, and the latter's two sons, Frigetius and Licentius, were placed under Augustine's tutelage. The talented Nebridius, leaving behind his fine paternal estate and his mother, made his way from Carthage that he might be near his former instructor. As was to be expected, Alypius found excuse to be in Milan also. The character of this future bishop excites admiration as well as interest.[1] One can not fail of conviction that in spite of his lapses, the young man Augustine was possessed of a sincere purpose, and unusual genius, in order to win to his side such a serious thinker as Nebridius, and a youth of such integrity as Alypius.

Of still greater significance was the reappearance, upon the scene, of Monica. Not a day had

---

[1] Confessions, VI, 16.

passed that tears and prayers had not given witness to the depth of her yearning and love. At length, alone, she dared the perils of the journey by sea, and displayed such unflinching courage that even the sailors found comfort in her assurance of safety. Great was her joy at finding her son released from alliance with the sect she dreaded and detested. Her counsels to him, blinded as they were by a pardonable wealth of affection, were not always the wisest. But her arrival in Milan was nevertheless opportune.

Milan was at this time, both in size and importance, the second city of Italy. Without the monumental majesty of Rome, it still presented all the outward marks of a gay capital. For there was the court and seat of empire of the youthful Valentinian, and to say that is to have the imagination crowded with pictures of soldiers, courtiers, palaces, public-squares and market-places alive with business, or thronged with listless idlers. Augustine's post was one of considerable honor and remuneration, and secured him entrance into the most cultured circles of Milan. He even intimates that social obligations to his more influential friends required much of his time.[2] One of his duties, evidently an irksome one with him, consisted in his preparation and delivery of a flattering discourse before the emperor. He was only one of the countless multitudes who confessed a reverence for their

---

[2] Confessions, VI, 18.

ruler whether they felt it or not; for the absoluteness of the emperor's power left no room for anything like freedom of speech.[8]

One of the painful things connected with Augustine's residence at Milan, was his attempt, or his mother's, to settle the question of his marriage. Seemingly there were two serious hindrances. First of all, could a man, bent on the highest attainment of wisdom and a life of honor, be burdened with conjugal cares? He concluded that "many men who are worthy of imitation have applied themselves to wisdom in the marriage state." The second hindrance was much more serious. It was a question of plain ethics, and the pity of it is that neither Augustine nor Monica treated it with any deep concern. With the unnamed woman he had been living in closest intimacy during fourteen years, and they had had one son born to them. Now that it was clearly manifest that a regular marriage would cause no interruption of his studies, he must look about for a wife. In this search he was ably supported by his mother. The mistress of so many years was out of the question; evidently she was of much lower birth, and it would have been "a miracle of self-sacrifice in the Roman world to have married her." But Monica had recourse to special revelations; might they not be effective in bringing to light the proper maiden? "We daily begged Thee that Thou wouldest by a vision disclose unto us something con-

---

[8] Cf. Bryce, The Holy Roman Empire, p. 21 f., for a discussion of the prerogatives of the emperors during the last three centuries of the empire.

cerning my future marriage; but Thou wouldest not."[4] It is wonderful that Augustine never discovered any inconsistency in the mere possibility of God's answering such prayers. But, dreams or no dreams, the suit must be pressed. At length a comfortably dowered girl of tender years was found, and as she "wanted two years of the marriageable age, she was waited for." All this was purely—or impurely—commercial. To complete the transaction, Augustine's former companion was directed back to Africa, whither she went "vowing never to know another man"—for which resolution one feels like commending her sound judgment. Had her lover displayed equal sense, we should be in a better position to sympathize with him when he bemoans his "racked, wounded, bleeding heart." Instead, he plunged headlong into a deeper mire of sensuality, not having the patience to wait for his nuptial-day. It may afford relief to some minds that society in that age had no frown for that sort of business—"did not reckon such connections indecent or profligate"—but to us it only increases the amazement that Christianity should be able to take a man, in the condition in which Augustine now found himself, and so thoroughly renovate him as to make him hate what he deemed a delightful necessity.

There were still other plans under consideration by Augustine and his set. They found it a vexa-

---

[4] Confessions, VI, 23.

tious thing to continue living as they had been. So they hit upon a kind of communistic scheme.[5] Romanianus was foremost in making the proposition and in supporting it by his great wealth. Two officers, charged with the household cares, were to have annual appointment, and the others to be left free from responsibility. A stumbling-block in the way of all this speedily made its appearance. As in the "Pantisocracy" of Southey and Coleridge, the woman question showed its head. But in this case she was the stumbling-block. Doubtless the primary object of the community had been to secure greater comfort to the members. But there seems to have been some notion of philosophic study. At any rate, shortly thereafter, Augustine was discussing with his closest friends the nature of good and evil, when the well-known contention of Epicurus about a happy life came up. Whereupon Augustine declared a life of pleasure might be defensible, were it not for the life hereafter. "For the fear of death and future judgment, amid all my fluctuations of opinion, never left my breast."[6]

These last words reveal one phase of Augustine's inner life, consideration of which purposely has been deferred till this time. He was not happy. He had set out to find wisdom, and at thirty, still pursuing more vulgar objects—wealth, worldly honor, and preferment—he confesses failure. On the Milanese streets he passes a poor beggar, "jok-

---

[5] Confessions, VI, 24.   [6] Confessions, VI, 26.

ing and joyous" with the fleeting pleasures a few small coins have bought him. This mendicant is happier than he. With all the felicities of the presence and love of dear friends, and in full indulgence of carnal appetites, he knows he has not yet come to inward peace. Manichæism he has discarded as a tattered, worthless garment; there are some philosophers that give him deeper satisfaction. He has turned to the Christian Scriptures, but has been repelled by their narrow literalism. Even the boasted systems of the Academicians provide him no firm footing.

Deeper than all this, of course, was Augustine's moral malady. He had been living far below his own ideal, and, as he looked hither and thither for a way out of the tangle, his soul was filled with despair and dread. But first of all must come an intellectual deliverance. Plainly there were two requisites. For one thing his conception of God must be clarified, and he must be impressed with the profound reality of a spiritual realm; otherwise there was no hope of his emerging from the gross realism of the Manichees. The other need was for an authority so masterful, as to give him an abiding certainty about the worth of the Scriptures, and as to oversweep his soul with the grandeur of the Christian Church. Of these two needs, the second was the first to be met. Augustine has made it very clear what he was seeking. In his book "On the Profit of Believing," written only a few years after the early experiences at Milan, and again in the "Confessions," he sets forth his mental struggles. Amidst all his wavering skepticism and distracting activities—scholars and mental drill, social demands and recreation—he could not forsake the quest of truth.[7] But the moment he launched upon the sea of conflicting thoughts, all was bewilderment. Where should he find certainty? For he was convinced that, so sure as there was a God, "He hath appointed some authority, whereon, resting as on a sure step, we may be lifted up to Him."[8] He says truly[9] that, at this critical moment, if there had been some one to teach him, he would have been found "most fervently disposed and very apt to learn." "For such a man whose will was weak and whose passions were powerful, whose strength lay chiefly in the life of the emotions, who had no canon for the recognition of truth, whose intellectual stability had been shaken by so many changes of opinion, there was but one resort at last—to fall back upon some external authority, if any such existed, powerful enough to subdue the intellect, to open up a channel for the emotions, and to hold the will to a definite purpose."[10]

As presenting more than a hint of the subtle, providential adjustments of life, there is absorbing

---

[7] Confessions, VI, 18 and 19. [8] On the Profit of Believing, 34.
[9] Ibid. 20.
[10] Professor A. V. G. Allen, The Continuity of Christian Thought, p. 146.

interest in the particular appearance, at this crisis, of the great Bishop Ambrose. Indeed, there is something significant in the way he began to loom so large upon Augustine's horizon that Milan and Ambrose became almost identical—"to Milan I come unto Ambrose the bishop." "To him was I unknowingly led by Thee, that by him I might knowingly be led to Thee."[11] With ecclesiastical dignity, but withal a fatherly warmth, the renowned bishop began his conquest of the polished young professor by winning him first to himself and to a new respect for the Church. All the world knew how Ambrose had risen, out of noble parentage, to become consular of practically all Upper Italy, and of his response to the call of the Church in a trying situation. All the refinements of his Roman birth and education, all the discrimination and alertness of a courageous governor whom every one respected and trusted, these he had brought with him to adorn the office which he began at once to fill with great wisdom, energy, and independence. Pre-eminently Ambrose was a pronounced Churchman. The man who later (390) was to accomplish the humiliation of an emperor,[12] had it in his power to awe questioning minds into submission, and to make them conscious, amidst the failures of the old institutions, of the supremacy of the forces of the Church. One finds no diffi-

---
[11] Confessions, V, 23.
[12] Theodosius. See Neander's Account, II, 180 f.

culty in imagining how this massive episcopal statesmanship would captivate a shrinking religious nature like Monica's. His words were out of heaven to her. When, one day, she went to the Church purposing to pay some respect to the memory of the martyrs and was halted by the porter who informed her that Ambrose had forbidden the ceremony, she submitted without the least hesitation.[13]

Augustine was already deeply under the spell of the bishop of Milan when Monica came to the city, and it was a source of joy to her. The personality and eloquent preaching and the atmosphere of Ambrose were irresistible. Augustine felt his prejudices against the Church melting away. There were other elements to aid this process. One was the splendor of the service of the Church at Milan. It was Ambrose who introduced musical features previously unknown in the worship of Italy, and himself composed hymns to be sung by the great congregations. Then in connection with this introduction of music occurred another event which must have had powerful weight with Augustine at this time. The predecessor of Ambrose was the Arian bishop, Auxentius. Consequently there was great excitement over the choice of Ambrose, a stout upholder of the Nicene faith. Valentinian I had approved, but his mother, Justina, stubbornly put her Arian priests in the field, demanding both

---

[13] Confessions, VI, 2; cf. City of God, VII, 27; also Ep. 36, 32, for further evidence of the influence of Ambrose on Monica.

the Portian basilica without the walls, and the new basilica, within. She supported her demands with an array of Gothic soldiery, and a threat of banishment. Then the loyalty of the people asserted itself. Surrounding the church and house of Ambrose, they kept guard, Monica among them, day and night. Thus without any physical force, Ambrose remained unyielding, and proved "how a great community, pervaded by an intense enthusiasm, can paralyze an administrative authority destitute of the elements of moral force."[14] Shortly after this, Ambrose clinched his claim to full supervision of the Churches, and finally repressed what Augustine calls "the feminine but royal fury," by an opportune discovery, and transference to the basilica of the bodies of two martyrs, Gervasius and Protasius. By means of these relics, a case of blindness and several cases of demon-possession are said by both Augustine[15] and Ambrose to have been cured. Whatever may be said of the "credibility" of these miracles, it is certain they were important to Augustine, as impressing him with the supernatural power of Christianity. Thus the popularity and power of Ambrose, the enrapturing wonder of choirs singing in antiphon, the reverent posture of the crowds of worshipers, and the sight of what were at least regarded as miracles, charmed the imagination of Augustine, and led him to enroll

---

[14] Principal Robert Rainy, The Ancient Catholic Church, p. 435 f.
[15] Confessions, XI, 16; City of God, XXII, 8; Sermon, 286, Sec. 4.

as a probationer in the Catholic Church, while he waited for further light.

It was from Ambrose also that he was to receive the first glimmerings of that light. Professor Harnack has pointed out that the most important influence of the East upon Ambrose lay in his reception of the allegorical method of exegesis,[16] and further, declares that Manichæism would hardly have been overcome in the West unless it had been confronted with the "Biblical alchemy" of the Greeks. One readily can see a special meaning in these words as applied to the problem which was perplexing Augustine. It was because he had come in contact with only a meager, "pedantically literal," and formless interpretation of the Scriptures, that the Manichæan charges against the Old Testament hitherto had seemed incapable of disproof. Ambrose brought relief into this entire situation. Not only did he "answer objections." He "drew aside the mystic veil," so that Augustine saw the possibility of deliverance from bondage to the letter. For, with all that was fantastic and overdrawn in the allegorical method, it had the merit of flooding the Scriptures with a new spirit, and this it was which drew Augustine to them at once.

But here, for the time being, the influence of Ambrose was at an end. He had made the Scriptures a new and attractive book for Augustine, and had crowded upon him the splendors of the visible

---

[16] History of Dogma, V, p. 32.

Church. For the rest he was too busy. Again and again the eager disciple sought a personal interview with the bishop. But always there was a crowd of hangers-on—some scrupulous Christian desiring advice in a matter of conscience, some unfortunate begging his intercession, others seeking settlement of a suit, a throng dependent upon his charity. And when they had all gone, and the exhausted head of the Church sat in his open court, snatching a few rare moments for mental refreshment out of some favorite book, the young men hardly dared venture beyond the door and a few hasty, reverential glances.[17] "Nothing is more touching," says the faithful Poujoulat,[18] "than this sight of the young Augustine, the future doctor of the Church, still a prey of doubts, entering the court of St. Ambrose, with discreet step and closed lips, throwing respectful looks upon the great bishop absorbed in some heavy reading, and soon after departing in silence, without having had the courage to disturb the quiet of the ecclesiastic." Accordingly, the surgings of spirit, the wonders and anxieties of mind, continued to possess Augustine. Whether Ambrose, at leisure, could have cleared the way to peace we can not tell. At all events, there was more truth to be had, and from another quarter.

---

[17] A trustworthy portrait of a busy bishop in a large city may be found in Kingsley's Hypatia, where the ordinary routine of Cyril of Alexandria is set forth. [18] Histoire de St. Augustin, I, p. 72.

CHAPTER VI.

THROUGH PLATO TO CHRIST.

As ALREADY indicated, one of the deepest needs of Augustine, during the period of mental disturbance, was a spiritualized conception of life and the world. However loosely the Manichæan view of things held him, its materialistic ideas of God and evil kept him in check. Until he found emancipation from these there could be no progress. It may be true that his skepticism was not radical. But he was beginning to lose hope, and he dreaded the outcome. The night of uncertainty to him meant profound misery and spiritual death. Professor Dods has pointed out a similarity between his experience in this respect and that of John Henry Newman.[1] But there was this difference—Newman professed never to have sinned against the light, while Augustine was conscious of deliberate moral failure, and his "crushing anxiety" grew out of this feeling as much as out of his doubts. To use his own confession, he was afraid of death.

But he could not utterly despair, because it was impossible for him to yield his belief in God. His grave concern now was to get beyond what the

---

[1] Lecture on St. Augustine delivered in Glasgow, Dec. 4, 1881.

preaching of Ambrose and his own reading of Scripture convinced him were wholly false and vulgar conceptions of Deity. He longed to be as sure of spiritual things as he was "that seven and three are ten." But he found it impossible to hold fast to the elusive idea of an unseen realm. He could not free his mind from "the flux of phenomena, the mysterious and harassing play of the transient." God could be thought of only as standing somewhere in space. Back to his mind, again and again, swept the crude and even disgusting notions which for so many years he had harbored there—God changeable and corruptible, God torn asunder, enduring loathsome pollution from mixture with matter, suffering like the trees and beasts and then gaining a painful freedom by their corruption, God the object of the successful onslaughts of evil. This last especially perplexed him. Plainly it made God a weakling—or a monster. For, if the vast wrong of the world was not here because of a divine debility, how else was one to account for it except as existing by divine direction? But did not Ambrose preach that it was man's will which was radically wrong?[2] Yes, but the problem was still a tangle—it always was for Augustine. Nevertheless he had rather remain in the dark than doubt the ultimate goodness of God. So he continued to

---

[2] This, of course, is only conjecture—i. e., so far as it applies to Augustine at this period. Still it seems to me well founded. Cf. many statements by Augustine himself, like Confessions, VII, 5; Fisher, History of Christian Doctrine, p. 187; Harnack, History of Dogma, p. 48 f.

read the Sacred Writings and to hang upon the sermons of Ambrose.

Augustine contracted a friendship at Milan with Manlius Theodorus, who became consul in 399. Theodorus was an ardent student of New Platonism, a philosophy, with leanings toward religion, which had reached its influences out from its Alexandrian cradle into various parts of the empire. Augustine soon fell to examining the teachings of the new school. With rather paltry gratitude he refers to "one inflated with most monstrous pride," giving him "certain books of the Platonists, translated from Greek into Latin." There is some doubt as to the exact authorship of these books, although one would not greatly err in picking out Plotinus as the one most directly responsible for the ideas they contained. Elsewhere Augustine hints at a familiarity with Jamblichus and Porphyry, and with his fellow-countryman Apuleius, but these made little advance upon the work of Plotinus, while to the "Enneads" of the latter it is not difficult to trace many of the conceptions which abound in Augustine.[3]

The New Platonism was a last determined effort of Hellenism to win the devotion of the old world. During this age, the absorbing question of philosophy was, whether there were two substances and distinct realms of being in the world, or whether

---

[3] This has been shown clearly by Professor A. H. Newman in his scholarly essay with which he introduces the Anti-Manichæan Writings of Augustine, Nicene and Post-Nicene Fathers, Vol. IV, p. 27 ff.

spirit and matter were essentially one. It was a
battle of Plato against the Stoics, of Theism against
Pantheism. What the New Platonists did was, first
to make alliance with both Stoic and Platonist
forces by offering a doctrine of evolution from the
supreme God to the lowest matter. Then (after
the manner of modern mediating theologies), in
order to make terms with all parties and organize
all, including "magic and marvels of legend," into
one, it must provide a basis for accepted forms of
religion. In this way there was offered to men a
doctrine of God—a triad Being made up of unity,
reason, and soul—and a theory of existence covering
all forms of life. The question of evil was
summarily dealt with: in reality there is none; it is
rather a lack of the intensely real One who is goodness,
and therefore can not have God for its author.
There was set forth also a doctrine of the impersonal
"Word," the Logos of the heretical Gnostics.
But concessions to Christianity, before whose militant
spirit New Platonism stood in wonder, were
distinctly avoided. Jesus was to be regarded only
as an austere man of large wisdom; the professions
of his followers were vulgar perversions of truth.
But the goal of all is the absorption of the individual
into God. "All that really is derives goodness
from Him; and in some wonderful way a consciousness
of God is obtainable which is victory,
emancipation, and blessedness. The progress
towards this goal and the attainment of it give life

THROUGH PLATO TO CHRIST. 71

a consecration and bathe it in a religious experience."[4]

One readily sees how Christian minds like Synesius, Nemesius, and Origen were stirred and deeply influenced by the idealism of the new philosophy, and how such restless spirits as Hypatia and Julian, in an age of shifting visions, could hazard life itself upon the truth of their doctrine. Augustine also confesses that the newly-discovered works of Plotinus kindled within him an incredible ardor.[5] They lifted before his vision a spiritual world. There he saw a God who answered his demand for an utmost good, mirrored some features of the Christian Trinity, and could by no means be limited to a narrow, fleshly prison. Thus his search for "incorporeal truth" was over. More than that, he had found an answer for his anxious query, oft-repeated: "Whence is evil?" For that which is but the negation of reality need not trouble the mind of any one; in fact, the remarkable ease with which he dismissed this mental difficulty is only a shade less wonderful than the readiness with which he began to see the many advantages which evil had made for the world. Then, in reminiscent mood, he turned, from pondering the frigid, ethereal Logos of the philosophers, to the Christ about whom they

---

[4] The reader is directed, for a fuller treatment, to Principal Rainy's luminous discussion, from which this last sentence is taken: Ancient Catholic Church, Chap. IX. Cf. also Sheldon, History of Christian Doctrine, p. 166 ff. In the Hypatia Kingsley has done some valuable reconstructing of the Neoplatonic philosophy.

[5] Against the Academicians, II, 5.

were silent, the "Word made flesh" of whom his mother had taught him in childhood, the Savior of men who in shame and humiliation bore the curse of the cross.[6] Thus he began to Christianize his ideals. In spite of him he could not lay hold on the Incarnation. Christ was still simply most excellent of men. But gradually the light was breaking in upon his forlorn soul. He even believed he saw "the unchangeable brightness," and beyond the possibility of doubt heard an inner voice bidding him go on.[7] For a brief season it seemed that the battle was won.

In truth the enemy had only retreated to prepare for a fresh attack. As Neander has aptly said: the Platonic theories were "demolished by the energy of life." "They ravished his intellectual vision," but they could give no victory over the flesh. From the mountain's wooded summit he had beheld the land of peace, but, alas! the way hither was dark and beset by the old foes. In this predicament he turned to Paul. This was the way of it: Into the Neoplatonic writings Augustine had been initiated by the translations and original works of the rhetorician Victorinus, that "aged man, most learned and highly skilled in the liberal sciences, who had read and weighed so many works of the philosophers, the instructor of so many senators, who also, as a monument of his excellent discharge of his office, had deserved and obtained a statue in

---

[6] Confessions, VII, 13, 14. [7] Ibid. VII, 16.

Through Plato to Christ. 73

the Roman Forum."[8] Harnack even considers it was from Victorinus that Augustine learned how to unite Neoplatonic speculation with Christianity. At all events, Victorinus had culled the characteristic thoughts of Paul, and we may assume that this is what led Augustine to examine more carefully the Pauline epistles.

At this point the moralist halts. It is enough for him that the promised land is already in sight. He can make nothing of the enigma of a Paul showing the way. "Let the pilgrim continue his secular way," he says, "heeding nothing of paths to heaven beyond a certain sobriety of life." Why should we seek for Augustine any more "conversion" than he had already? The answer is near at hand. The pressure towards progress was in himself. What he had was of value, but it could not satisfy him. There was an inward unrest, a life-and-death struggle to subdue the sensual to the ideal. It was not the allurements of secular life which held him. These he could give up; the thought of wealth and honor had ceased to charm. But, frankly he bares the truth, "very tenaciously was I held by the love of women." With the fatherland in full view, and the dogged insistence of corrupt passions a powerful reality, the meaning of the great apostle could not be mistaken—the war between flesh and spirit was no phantasm.

Fortunately there were friends to whom he

---

[8] Confessions, VIII, 3.

might turn. And he could have chosen none more sagacious than Simplicianus, whom both Ambrose and Augustine delighted to address as "father." The aged saint did not rebuke. Like his Master at Sychar, he followed the lead which the occasion presented. Augustine, in making a clean breast of his wanderings, mentioned his indebtedness to Victorinus. This was a golden moment for Simplicianus, for it was he who had stopped Victorinus short in the midst of his "thundering eloquence" in behalf of heathen gods, and had led him to a humble confession of Christ. Openly, to the amazement of all Rome and the joy of the Church, Victorinus had made declaration of his choice of The Way. Consequently, by a law of Julian, he had been forbidden, as a Christian, any longer to teach rhetoric. Upon hearing this recital, the ardent Augustine "burned to imitate him."[9] But forthwith the conflict became more tense. "With the baggage of the world was I burdened, as when in slumber; and the thoughts wherein I meditated upon Thee were like unto the efforts of those desiring to awake, who, still overpowered with a heavy drowsiness, are again steeped therein."[10] "And to Thee showing me on every side that what Thou saidst was true, I, convicted by the truth, had nothing at all to reply, but the drawling and drowsy words: 'Presently, lo, presently.'"

---

[9] This entire story of Victorinus is worth reading for its dramatic interest and picture of a noble spirit. See the Confessions, VIII, 3–9.

[10] Confessions, VIII, 12.

Alypius was sharing with Augustine this period of anxious sorrow. One would be barren of all feeling not to be moved by this picture of the two young men, under firm seizure of the Spirit of God, seeking release almost daily in the great Church,[11] being swept from their sensual pleasures while wilfully holding them fast. To them there came one day an imperial officer, Potitianus, who was one of their own country. As they talked, the eyes of the visitor lighted upon a book, which to his surprise was no other than the writings of the Apostle Paul. Potitianus being a baptized Christian, it was natural that his conversation should turn to religious themes. From speaking of Antony, he passed to a description of the Egyptian monks, their wilderness retirement and unselfishness, while Augustine sat enraptured. At Triers, on a certain afternoon, so this Christian officer went on to relate, two of his comrades had been so deeply impressed by the devotion of Antony, that they resolved to follow his example. Their affianced brides, thereupon, also dedicated themselves to God. While Potitianus was weaving the threads of his tale, Augustine was burning with shame to think how cowardly and sordid he had been. Other weaker ones had done in a trice what he shrank from as if it were death.

---

[11] For this reason I can not agree with Professor Allen that Augustine's conversion was merely into the Latin Church. It was something more. We must not, in the interests of a theory, depreciate the full movement of Augustine's course, step by step, till he claimed Christ as his. Cf. Continuity of Christian Thought, p. 149.

He cast his eye backwards. There were his mother's example and prayers, the pitiful meshes of Manichæism, the higher note of the "Hortensius," Ambrose, Plotinus, Paul, these later instances of heroic faith—Victorinus, Antony, the comrades of Potitianus. Was he, the finished rhetorician, the prodigal, to fall down beaten in the dust? He seized upon Alypius. "What is wrong with us? what is this? What heardest thou? The unlearned rise up and take heaven, and we, with our learning, and wanting heart, see where we wallow in flesh and blood!" In his excitement he flung himself into the garden. He knew now that all that remained was to choose unflinchingly the only course opened to him—"to will it resolutely and thoroughly, not to stagger and sway about this way and that, a changeable and half-wounded will, with one part falling as another rose." No words ever can take the place of Augustine's own thrilling ones in describing the momentous scenes which followed:

"Thus was I sick and tormented, accusing myself far more severely than was my wont, tossing and turning me in my chain till that was utterly broken, whereby I now was but slightly, but still was held. And Thou, O Lord, pressedst upon me in my inward parts by a severe mercy, redoubling the lashes of fear and shame, lest I should again give way, and that same slender remaining tie not being broken off, it should recover strength, and enchain me the faster. For I said mentally, 'Lo, let it be done now, let it be done now.' And as I spoke, I all but came to a resolve. I all but did it, yet I did it not. Yet fell I not back to my old condition, but took up my position hard by, and drew breath. And I tried again, and wanted but very little of reaching it, and then all but touched and grasped it; and yet came not at it, hesitating to die unto death, and to live unto life; and the worse, whereto I had been habituated, prevailed more with me than the better, which I had not tried.

"The very toys of toys, and vanities of vanities, my old mistresses, still enthralled me; they shook my fleshly garment, and whispered softly, 'Dost thou part with us? And from that moment shall we no more be with thee forever?' Yet they did delay me, so that I hesitated to burst and shake myself free from them, and to leap over whither I was called,—an unruly habit saying to me, 'Dost thou think thou canst live without them?'"

"But now it said this very faintly; for on that side towards which I had set my face, and whither I trembled to go, did the chaste dignity of continence appear unto me, cheerful, but not dissolutely gay, honestly alluring me to come and doubt nothing, and extending her holy hands, full of a multiplicity of good examples, to receive and embrace me. There were there so many young men and maidens, a multitude of youth and every age, grave widows and ancient virgins, and Continence herself in all, not barren, but a fruitful mother of children of joys, by Thee, O Lord, her husband. And she smiled on me with an encouraging mockery, as if to say, 'Canst not thou do what these youths and maidens can? Or can one or other do it of themselves, and not rather in the Lord their God? The Lord their God gave me unto them. Why standest thou in thine own strength, and so standest not? Cast thyself upon Him; fear not, He will not withdraw that thou shouldest fall; cast thyself upon Him without fear, He will receive thee, and heal thee.' And I blushed beyond measure, for I still heard the muttering of those toys, and hung in suspense.

"But when a profound reflection had, from the secret depths of my soul, drawn together and heaped up all my misery before the sight of my heart, there arose a mighty storm, accompanied by as mighty a shower of tears. Which, that I might pour forth fully, with its natural expressions, I stole away from Alypius; for it suggested itself to me that solitude was fitter for the business of weeping. I flung myself down, how, I know not, under a certain fig-tree, giving free course to my tears. And, not indeed in these words, yet to this effect, spake I much unto Thee,—'How long, Lord? Wilt Thou be angry forever? O, remember not against us former iniquities;' for I felt that I was enthralled by them. I sent up these sorrowful cries,—'How long, how long? To-morrow, and

Through Plato to Christ.

to-morrow? Why not now? Why is there not this hour an end to my uncleanness?'

"I was saying these things and weeping in the most bitter contrition of my heart, when, lo, I heard the voice as of a boy or girl, I know not which, coming from a neighboring house, chanting, and oft repeating, 'Take up and read; take up and read.' So, restraining the torrent of my tears, I rose up, interpreting it no other way than as a command to me from heaven to open the book, and to read the first chapter I should light upon. So quickly I returned to the place where Alypius was sitting; for there had I put down the volume of the apostles, when I rose thence. I grasped, opened, and in silence read that paragraph on which my eyes first fell,—'Not in rioting and drunkenness, not in chambering and wantonness, not in strife and envying; but put ye on the Lord Jesus Christ, and make not provision for the flesh to fulfill the lusts thereof.'[12] No further would I read, nor did I need; for instantly, as the sentence ended—by a light, as it were, of security infused into my heart —all the gloom of doubt vanished away."

The far-remote, unintelligible, unconcerned "Word" had been transformed before his eyes, by his own obedience into a regnant Christ, who now drew near, warm with life and sympathy. "Startled, shattered, paralyzed," as he had been by the message of the Apostle, he arose with a singular

---

[12] Rom. xiii, 13, 14.

calm resting upon him, and like Andrew to Simon Peter, made known his new joy to Alypius.

"And he thus disclosed to me what was wrought in him, which I knew not. He asked to look at what I had read. I showed him; and he looked even further than I had read, and I knew not what followed. This it was, verily, 'Him that is weak in the faith, receive ye;' which he applied to himself, and discovered to me. By this admonition was he strengthened; and by a good resolution and purpose, very much in accord with his character (wherein, for the better, he was always far different from me), without any restless delay he joined me. Thence we go in to my mother. We make it known to her,—she rejoiceth. We relate how it came to pass,—she leapeth for joy, and triumpheth, and blesseth Thee, who art able to do exceeding abundantly above all that we ask or think."

CHAPTER VII.

CASSICIACUM.

It is impossible to determine what were the immediate effects of Augustine's conversion. One has no difficulty in perceiving, however, that his reformation was more than skin-deep. With sudden, superhuman resolve, as if by magic, he was able to throw off his inveterate delight in trifles. "The gnawing cares of seeking and getting" forever were left behind, and in their place there arose a new and all-absorbing "brightness," "riches," "health," the Lord his God.[1]

But there was not to be such instantaneous release from the "talker's trade." Deep-seated as was his disgust with the deceitful mockeries of his profession, he conceived various reasons for quiet self-restraint. The vintage vacation was but a few weeks distant. It might seem like undue and rather pompous self-protrusion to resign at once. Fortunately (so Augustine considered it) there was, for his approaching resignation, another excuse, which would tend to allay the resentment of his patrons. During the summer he had become conscious of a pain-

---
1 Confessions IX, 1.

ful difficulty in breathing. This indication that his lungs were weakening so greatly alarmed him that he was already planning to give up his literary labors for a rest, when his happy conversion opened to him a rare vista of leisurely service of God.

Accordingly, Augustine's withdrawal from public duties, at the end of the scholastic year, occasioned no unusual comment. His friend Verecundus owned a country-house out of Milan a few leagues at the village of Casciago, which seems beyond dispute to be the "Cassiciacum" of the "Confessions." At the generous suggestion of Verecundus, Augustine turned to this retreat. Removed as it was from the "fret of the world," it seemed to him like a paradise of realized hopes. The little town itself lay at the foot of the mountains in a fertile, grassy country, as the name suggests. On the summit of a hill travelers still see the ancient palace of a former family of nobles, marking the spot where the house of Verecundus was located. A stream, gushing down from Mount Sirtori, trickles over the rocks of the hill, and gathering into cascades, winds down into a shaded gorge. Like Saul of Tarsus, finding the Son of God, as Dr. Alexander Whyte declares, under the Mount of God in the eloquent silences of Arabia, Augustine needed this autumn and winter of isolation in order to work over his thinking and get adjusted to his vision. Besides, it gave to him and his companions an opportunity to put into tangible form their dream of a philosophic community.

For a picture of life at Cassiciacum during these few months we depend mostly upon the philosophical treatises which Augustine composed there. It was a period of tranquillity, but of earnest thought. Plain living and high thinking were the rule. The sons of Romanianus were present for instruction. Alypius, who had shared with Augustine the struggles of the last months in Milan, felt himself under agreeable constraint to continue as comrade of his master's solitude. A compatriot from Thagaste, Evodius, who had renounced the service of the empire upon becoming a Christian, also joined the group. The others were all relatives of Augustine—Navigius his brother, two cousins, Rusticus and Lastidianus, the boy Adeodatus, and Monica. To the latter was assigned the care of the household, but she found time to take some part in the discussions.

These discussions took place, in fair weather, beneath the shade of a tree in a near-by meadow. If the disputants were driven indoors they had recourse to the baths. These were supplied with water from a little aqueduct, which, in turn, was fed from the stream called Canbalionum. In the bath of the Romans, as is well known, were spacious rooms for recreation and quiet. Here the searchers for truth might carry on their conversations without interruption. One of Augustine's admiring biographers has compared him to an eagle, teaching his eaglets to fly, putting his strength beneath them, to bear them up, or to direct them in their flight. There is some truth in the figure. Licentius, for example, was a dreamy novice. He was eager enough for flight, but the serious moral and religious realm held few allurements for him. He felt the tinglings of an inflated poetic fancy. Indeed, so far did he swerve from the strenuous course of the parent eagle, as to break forth in rhythmic praises of the loves of Pyramus and Thisbe. Augustine was gravely concerned. But he lived to see even the aspiring Licentius find his wings and "the steep ascent of heaven."[2] The others were not so intractable. Adeodatus, a lad of not quite fifteen years, showed unusual fondness and skill for the business of empyrean-climbing. Monica, with a somewhat more awestruck admiration, joined the rest in their loyalty to the suggestions of Augustine.

But Augustine himself was hardly more than a learner. Much as we are impressed by the vigor of thought displayed in the discourses, we can not but note how gradual was their author's break with the old intellectual atmosphere. Cicero, Plotinus, Plato, Pythagoras, are the master-minds one finds ruling the treatises composed at Cassiciacum. On

---

[2] McCabe has an interesting note in which he calls attention to Lanciani's record of the discovery of the body of Licentius in St. Lorenzo at Rome in 1862. It is evident that he attained his ambition of senatorial rank and died a Christian. St. Augustine and His Age, p. 182.

the other hand, the grandeur of the Christian system burst in upon these philosophic studies with only a pale light. Ambrose, upon being consulted, had said, "read Isaiah;" but the prophet had seemed to Augustine dull and unintelligible. So he gave his attention to the Psalms. They continued through life to afford him consolation and guidance. To his penetrating allegorical faculty every page of the Psalms yielded some lineament in the portrait of Christ. Nor can we doubt that Augustine entered upon his new religious experience with the most cordial zeal. Prayer and praise mingled with sorrow over the hapless past and earnest aspiration for a humbler, nobler future. But the spirit of the place, however Christianized, was still Greek.

There can be no clearer understanding of the entire situation of this newest academy than through a study of the literary results of the conferences together. One day Augustine gave his pupils a copy of the "Hortensius" to read. All were seated beneath the broad-spreading tree in the meadow. It was a rare autumn day. The ever-present shorthand reporter stood near, waxen tablets and stylus in hand, ready to take down for preservation all that was said or done. Following his literary instinct, Augustine afterwards revised these notes in longhand, retaining the form of the discussion, and breaking up the heavy periods with notes on incidents of the day. Thus we have the readable books, "Against the Academicians," which are affectionately dedicated to Romanianus, and grew out of the examination of the book of Cicero. The point at issue was the academic contention that it is impossible to arrive at the truth, though one may be happy in pursuit of it. Licentius put in his plea in behalf of the Academics; for him it was a constant joy to be opening the eyes upon new worlds of truth. Trigetius had mixed up in the affairs of the world, and he had concluded with precision that if one could be happy without reaching the truth, there was no use making the quest. Augustine made it his duty to keep the debate in proper poise. He proffered a definition of a happy life—a life conformed to the best and most perfect in man, namely, the reason. Resting in this Platonic notion of rational truth, he found certainty enough. As for the other method of knowledge, authority, he was satisfied with what he had in Christ. Thus, he declared, he could not despair of finding wisdom at last, especially as he was but thirty-two, and bent upon the search with all his soul. In his old age Augustine looked back upon this scene with some misgivings. He felt he had given too much credit to the Greeks. But one can hardly fail to observe that, Christian as he was, the skillful antagonist of the Academics had been with Plato and learned of him.

A birthday was an affair of some moment in the empire. Much the same ado accompanied its observance as in our day. There were complimentary gifts and congratulations from friends, and generally also a time of feasting. As the Ides of November was the anniversary of Augustine's birth, he promised his friends "a feast of soul." But first there must be a modest banquet—modest, since frugality is said to have presided over all the repasts at Cassiciacum. They "satisfied hunger without clogging the vivacity of the mind." The intellectual feast was made up of a prolonged discussion of "The Happy Life." When the question of the existence of evil came up, Augustine turned his artillery upon the Manichees. His mother, who on the first day had brought the conference to an abrupt close by an insistent mid-day appeal for all hands to exchange the shade of the tree for the delights of the table, made some forcible remarks, seconded by Augustine, when the discussion was resumed at the baths. Their conclusion was that they alone are blessed who have what they desire, provided they desire the good. Little importance can be attached to this work except as it is an index of the bent of Augustine's mind, and his special fondness for the problems of evil.

There is much more lively interest in the work which followed. It was Augustine's habit, after evening prayers, to surrender himself to deep and long-continued meditations. One night, as he lay philosophizing thus, his attention was attracted by the gurgling of the stream which ran behind the baths not far from the house. As he listened to the soft, irregular murmur, his mind sought the cause of the irregularity, and from that passed to pondering on order and the lack of order in the universe. He became confused, like many another, in trying to establish the truth of a uniform "reign of law." Doubtless he was glad of the companionship of even the young versifier Licentius, who was busy at this critical moment belaboring an unfortunate mouse which had so far broken the order of things, as to venture into the room where the master and his pupils were resting. Licentius suggested that the swirl of the stream was nothing new to him; often it had quickened his sensitive imagination. Trigetius awakened at this point. It was an opportunity glowing with dialectic possibilities, and the diligent teacher could not conscientiously allow it to pass. So he kept the theme warm during the remainder of the night. Even Licentius maintained a wakeful interest, unmindful for the time being of the charms of his Calliope. The strenuous life of the seminary was beginning to tell upon him. At the baths next morning the discussion was renewed. On their way thither they witnessed another, more ugly, break in nature, a spirited cock-fight. The two boys, not being able to shake off entirely the fascinations of the Coliseum, looked on with evident delight, and Augustine hastened to prepare graphic details of the scene. Strangely enough the sober bishop of Hippo made no alteration of these in the "Retractations." All that day and several that followed, until Augustine was thoroughly fatigued, were given to the elucidation of the question of a mysterious, divine stream of influence running through all things. Such was the origin of the book "On Order," a pretentious treatise, with leanings toward the Christian thought of Providence, and with a Neoplatonic background.

In addition to several letters (the first we have of Augustine's), which throw welcome light upon the happy life at Cassiciacum, there remains one work of two books to which some critical notice must be given. It is a Platonic dialogue between Augustine and Reason, and is given the title "Soliloquies." The two things which attracted Augustine were the immortality of the soul and the true conception of God. The former truth was conclusive to him from his observation of the immutability of reason as compared with the break-up of the world. With graceful eloquence he makes his leisurely argument for the things which abide, and unfolds the conditions of ascending to the clear vision of God. Halting logic there may be, but never, in the confusion of later struggles, did Augustine rise higher than in this quiet meditation upon the devotional truths which had now subdued his passions and brought his soul into harmony with God.[3]

In the "Soliloquies," Augustine appears undecided as to the direction of his future life. But

---

[3] It is in the Soliloquies that one finds the rudiments of the philosophic starting-point of Descartes: "I think and therefore am."

his mind had turned back often to Milan and the Church. In the spring of 387, therefore, the household of friends relinquished their life of study and returned to the city. It was necessary for all who were to be baptized on Easter Sunday to declare their purpose at the beginning of Lent. Then followed a period of training in matters of Christian faith, and examination in "the scrutinies." Augustine was not exempt from this preparation. But he employed his time also in literary effort, producing the treatise "On the Immortality of the Soul." It was intended as a complement to the "Soliloquies."

By Easter the candidates were thought to be in a sufficiently humble frame of mind. Alypius indeed had demonstrated the depth of his devotion by treading "the frozen soil of Italy with naked feet." On the eve of Easter, April 24th, Augustine was formally ushered into the Church by the rite of baptism, Bishop Ambrose administering the sacrament. The youthful Adeodatus, and Alypius were baptized at the same time. A popular, but unfounded legend has it that, at the close of the service, the "Te Deum Laudamus" sprang into inspired existence through the lips of Ambrose and Augustine. The truth is that, by the impressive singing of the hymns and canticles, Augustine was rapt into a deeper devotion to the Church—a devotion which grew richer and sterner in the years immediately to follow, as he broke gradually away from the life of contemplation and gave himself to a life of service.

SECOND PERIOD

FROM EASTER, 387, TO AUGUST 28, 430

CHAPTER VIII.

BACK TO AFRICA.

THAT Augustine's moral rescue was complete, appears in the readiness with which he turned his back upon the old life. Accompanied by Alypius, Evodius, his brother, mother, and son, he set out for Africa. At Ostia, a busy watering-place and commercial center, being at the mouth of the Tiber and the port of Rome, the little company paused for rest after the fatiguing journey from Milan. They were pleasantly established in a house removed from the noise of the town. A somewhat idealized painting by Ary Scheffer,[1] and the familiar account in the "Confessions," have made memorable Augustine's last conversation with his mother.[2] Monica, overjoyed, felt now she might depart in peace. Her one desire had been satisfied—her son was a Catholic Christian. Surely there was nothing else for which to tarry. Within five days she was stricken with a fatal fever.

It was about four years since Augustine had deserted his mother at Carthage. During that time

---
[1] An excellent reprint may be found as a frontispiece to Poujoulat's Histoire de St. Augustin, Paris, 1866.
[2] Confessions IX, Chap. X.

their relations apparently were of the closest nature. Monica was reared in a Christian home. With her sisters she was left under the care of a maidservant, who sought diligently to train the daughters according to strict rules. This discipline, however, did not suffice to save her from sly peculations of wine when sent to the cellar for the daily supply from the family cask. Augustine describes, with filial admiration, how his mother was cured of this habit, and how she grew up to be a model of sobriety, pious devotion, gentleness, and patience. We may not go so far as one branch of the Church in the veneration we give to this godly woman.[3] But no one can estimate the debt which Augustine himself owed to his praying mother. She had a deal of shrewd, sagacious wisdom, and a courageous spirit. And it is true that the Church has canonized many women of inferior type. Among the broken columns and forlorn ruins of modern Ostia one is directed to a chapel which, tradition declares, marks the site of the house where Augustine and Monica parted. Although she had been careful to prepare a burial-place for herself beside that of her husband in Thagaste, she now saw the hopelessness of her plan. "Nothing is far to God," she said resignedly; "nor need I fear lest He should be ignorant at the end of the world of the place where He is to raise me up."[4] Upon her death

---

[3] For an example of this extreme reverential respect see Poujoulat, I, p. 142 ff. [4] Confessions, IX, 27, 28.

a few days later, and her simple burial, Augustine suffered a quiet but persistent grief. Relief came with sleep and the recollection of a hymn of Ambrose,—"Deus Creator omnium." But fresh remembrance of the tender love of his dead mother set free the tears, which he begs us not to deride, since they were in behalf of one who for many years wept bitter tears for him.

From Ostia, Augustine made his way back to Rome. It is difficult to assign any other reason for this change of plan, except that Africa was in a turmoil owing to an expedition by the usurper Maximus, and Augustine decided to wait till the campaign was over. Already he had adopted the long dark robe of the monks, with hood and leathern girdle. Doubtless he regarded the great city in a much different spirit from what he did when he went there to become teacher of rhetoric. All the world looked strangely new to him. There was a duller hue to the glitter and grossness of the mistress city; not because the gayety was gone, but because it had lost its charm. Jerome had taken his inbe by other than severely monastic methods. But the enthusiasm for Jerome's ideas had not died out among his followers in some of the higher society of Rome, and with these it may be Augustine found a refuge. Not till more than a score of years had passed did he turn his attention to the religion which had dominated the empire for centuries. But the former worship was dying hard. The doughty Symmachus had not yet abandoned the contest. Many pagans were still to be found in important civil offices. Libanius, when a demolition of temples was rampant among fanatical monks and priests, uttered a notable plea in defense of the temple cult. And the Emperor Theodosius, in a law of 386, presupposes a tolerant spirit towards both temples and heathen priests. Nevertheless, ecclesiastical insistence was beginning to tell. Everywhere the sacrificial flames burned lower. In 388, while Augustine was in Rome, the heathen portion of the senate besought Theodosius to restore certain revenues and rights to the colleges of priests. The emperor seems to have wavered. But a sharp letter from Ambrose brought him to his senses, and the request was denied.

Of all this Augustine has nothing to say. At Rome he was busy with literary labors. His one concern seems to have been to demolish the pretensions of his old friends, the Manichees. The sect, in spite of inceasingly rigid opposition from the imperial power, especially Valentinian (in 372) and Theodosius (in 381), propagated their doctrines in secret, and with considerable success. They gloried in persecution. Under the mask of an apparently unbending morality, they won respect. By proclaiming a mysterious element in their doctrine and symbols, they had become the most dangerous foe of the Christian faith. It is not surprising, therefore, that Augustine, in the ardor of his new-found faith, should direct his energies against "the monstrous tenets of the Manichæans." He took up his attack first in a series of dialogues between himself and Evodius, under the title, "On the Greatness of the Soul." In this work the arguments are lined up in favor of the spiritual nature and immortal destiny of the soul, together with a philosophical view of its beginnings, aspirations, and powers. About the same time also he began what has been called "an admirable Pelagian treatise," "On Free Will." In reality, it is an attempt to reduce the possible origins of evil down to one, the freedom of human will. It ought to be said that Augustine never receded from this position. His later contentions against Pelagius were of an altogether different kind. His anti-Manichæan position, that moral evil is not a creation of God, did not afford the Pelagians a stable ground of attack upon him, however minutely they searched for one in these earlier writings.

Of deeper significance were the more direct assaults upon his foes, in the works entitled "On the Morals of the Church" and "On the Morals of the Manichees." Though these were not published till later, we are told in the "Retractations" (I. 7) they were written at Rome. The immediate occasion of their writing was his impatience with "the vaunting of the Manichæans about their pretended and misleading abstinence, in which, to deceive the inexperienced, they claim superiority over true Christians, to whom they are not to be compared." As might be supposed, therefore, the two works stand in contrast. He has no trouble in tearing to shreds the symbols and dogmas of the Manichees, although it may be questioned whether he is equally happy in his arraignment of their "shameless mysteries," their immoral practices, and especially their disgraceful conduct laid bare in Rome.[5] In the other work, Augustine seeks to make clear the nature of Christian virtue. With glowing phrase, he pictures the devotion of the multitudes who, in depth of desert, subsisting on coarse fare, passing their days in contemplation of the Divine beauty and in religious conference, present an unanswerable challenge to the hypocrisies of the Manichæans. Then he passes to the Cenobite monks who live in the cities. One can without difficulty detect in all this what was uppermost in Augustine's thought during the year in Rome. There was forming in his mind a monastic ideal, which was soon to take very definite form.

The forces of Maximus in Africa proved no match for those of the emperor. Peace was soon restored, and Augustine was free to carry out his original design of continuing at Thagaste the sort of life which had been begun at Cassiciacum. He

---

[5] It is fruitless to go into this controversy further. Anybody who reads Augustine's disclosures, e. g., in the treatise under question, Chaps. XVIII-XX, can not doubt that, if he exaggerates, he also has plenty of basis for all his facts.

and his friends, however, were detained for a brief time at Carthage. They were received by a devotedly pious man, Innocentius, "ex-advocate of the deputy prefecture." Still fresh in his memory were the miraculous occurrences at Milan. He was, therefore, more than naturally responsive to what he saw and heard at Carthage. Innocentius was being treated for a dangerous disease, for which he had already undergone an operation. After a period of anxious waiting and intense pain, it was discovered another operation was necessary. Augustine himself was present the night before, as were two bishops, Amelius and Uzali, and all prayed earnestly for the recovery of the unfortunate man. Great was their amazement, next day, at finding the trouble entirely at an end. The ingenious McCabe, with his usual irony, attempts to involve Augustine in intentional deceit at this point. He begins, by citing a work of Augustine's written some two years later. In this book, "On True Religion," "there is wise appreciation of the work of reason in establishing the preliminary truths of faith," seeing that miracles were no longer wrought in its interest. As a matter of fact, Augustine's purpose in the treatise, as elsewhere, was to show that history was one of the foundations of the true religion, and he concludes that such miracles as the past, especially the Apostolic period, produced, must no longer be expected. This must be his meaning in the "Retractations" where he declares, commenting on this passage, that he intended to say "the same miracles" were not performed in his day. It is completely to overdraw one's bow to conclude, as McCabe does, that "Augustine smiled at his host's miracles in 388, and only learned to appreciate them years after."

Another evidence that the same author is more interested in making an amusing case for himself than in correctly representing Augustine, is found in rather a ludicrous result of his own misrepresentations. In attempting to put in a bad light most of the hagiographic "lives" of Augustine, he says, with very ingenuous glee, that "they only relate two miracles" (he might at least have spared his grammar the violence), "whereas Augustine gives three in the 'City of God.'" Even a casual reading of the attestations of Augustine would discover four. One of these, in the light of present-day knowledge, is exceedingly refreshing. A gouty doctor, about to be baptized, was visited in dreams by black woolly-haired imps who inflicted acute pains by dancing on his feet, and warned him not to be baptized that year. But he persisted, and in baptism was rid not only of gout, but also of the little devils. There can be no doubt of the eagerness with which Augustine received these examples of "miraculous power." But it would be blindness for us to accept them upon the very slight evidence which is given. In truth, as Professor Fisher has shown, the evidence vanishes on close scrutiny. "We miss the sobriety of the Gospel narratives." The worship of relics, prayer to saints and martyrs, and other superstitions had fastened themselves on the Church, and these, together with a rather picturesque style of rhetoric, account for the many alleged miracles, while others are traceable to purely natural causes.[6]

We are to think of Augustine as spending the next three years in a monastery, established in the former house of his father at Thagaste. His notions of monasticism came from various sources. Ambrose and Jerome made their contributions; but the Cenobites, already referred to, were probably the real model. Augustine did not go to the lengths which brought down upon Jerome the denunciations of Rome's mighty. He came to Thagaste bent upon purging the monastic idea of those out-breaking fanaticisms and wild excesses which he knew had grown up in Africa from the roots of Tertullianism. He sold his other property and endowed the monastery. His friends, Alypius and Evodius, continued with him. The problem of women was no longer a snare. Without exception, none were permitted to lodge beneath the same roof. A life of study and prayer became "the rule of St. Augustine." Out of these beginnings, it must be

---

[6] In his Grounds of Theistic and Christian Belief, Professor George P. Fisher makes a searching and sane examination of the entire question of alleged miracles in the early age of the Church, with special reference to Augustine's long list. He concludes that "the evidence for most of the post-apostolic miracles which the Fathers advert to melt away on examination."

noted, grew the important Augustinian order of monks, at length to produce a Luther.

It is hardly fair to say that this first Augustinian brotherhood was wholly unpractical. To be sure there was a spirit of broadest democracy in the conditions of admission. A majority of the monks had been slaves, or tillers of the soil, or lowly artisans; for, it was argued, had not many noble men risen from the humblest ranks? "This pious and holy thought, accordingly, causeth that even such be admitted as bring no proof of a change of life for the better."[7] Why? Because of the impossibility of determining their motive. Accordingly there grew up a class of idle, crafty, casuistical fellows, who, under the garb of monastics, roamed about the country, a menace and a nuisance. Being respected they strolled here and there, trading "reliques" trumped up for the purpose, or pretending they were on a visit to relatives. Everywhere they made capital of the outward impression of sanctity. Augustine had to confess, after a few years, that their hypocrisy often was exposed by detected frauds and sensual indulgence.[8] All this grew partly out of Augustine's more moderate and idyllic view of an ascetic life, and partly out of laxity in discipline. Nevertheless, he saw the dangers of idleness and license, with men who formerly had been burdened by heavy labors and close restraints. Accordingly, he was unwilling to discard entirely the obligation

---

[7] On the Work of Monks, chap. 25.   [8] Ibid. chap. 36.

BACK TO AFRICA.

to manual labor. Then there was, upon many of these men who had known only the coarser side of life, a softening influence, which counted for much in developing some of the Church's most respected leaders. It must be admitted, however, that the bad results outweighed the good, and that the seed planted in Augustine's "Spiritual Seminary" was destined to bear an amazingly unwholesome fruitage.

For a proper idea of Augustine's occupations at Thagaste, we must look to the letters. One thing that impresses us is, that the busy monk had not shut all light and beauty out of his heart. Among the most tender relations of his life were those with Nebridius. The passing reference in the "Confessions," and the letters[9] give us entrance into a friendship of rare sympathy and sweetness. Nebridius was unable to make his home at the monastery, but returned to his home near Carthage, where he was seized with a wasting disease which soon resulted in his death. Augustine kept him cheered; his messages, the sick man said, were to his ears "like Christ, like Plato, like Plotinus." In another letter, Augustine becomes playful. Discussing the size of the planets, he remarks upon the prodigious statue of Nævius. "By the way, I think you have been just too eager to discover some man to match him; and when you did not succeed, have resolved to make me stretch out my letter so as to

---

[9] Confessions, IX, 5 and 6; also Eps. 3, 4, 5, 6, 7, 8, 9, 10, 11, 13, 14.

rival his dimensions." He concludes by writing: "I beg you be content with what I have written, although I have already outdone Nævius himself." One must not paint the portrait of Augustine the monk in too somber hues.[10]

From another part of the correspondence with Nebridius, it appears that the people of Thagaste took advantage of Augustine's genius and set him up as a kind of justice. But he had little liking for it. Besides a vigorous correspondence he devoted himself to authorship. The Manichæans had not ceased to disturb him. Their stubborn hostility to the Old Testament led Augustine at length to venture upon a defense of Genesis, in which he resorted to the Ambrosian method of allegorical explanation of the stories of creation and the fall. This was only the initial step of later works on the same subject, finally issuing in the large commentary on "A Literal Rendering of Genesis,"—a work which in our day has no practical value, and only an antiquarian interest. Another treatise was begun, but not completed, "On Music." A frank statement of the value of this work occurs in a letter (101) written several years later to Bishop Memor, who wished a copy. Augustine confesses that the first five books, on rhythm, are a sort of labyrinthal maze from which the puzzled bishop would find it difficult to extricate himself. Augustine also had a lively passage at arms with a grammarian of Ma-

---

[10] Cf. also Ep. 4: "I am yet but a boy, though perhaps, as we say, a promising boy, rather than a good-for-nothing."

daura. This old man, Maximus, wrote to ask why there was anything unfitting in the market-place of his town being occupied by statues of the gods, and who the Christian God actually was. It is perfidious to say, as one of Augustine's biographers has done, that his reply is "harsh" and a "bitter, contemptuous attack on the poor Olympians." He merely calls upon Maximus to treat seriously, and not jocularly, a serious subject, and takes the occasion to expose the follies of heathen worship. Of the work "On the True Religion," addressed to Romanianus with the hope of winning him to Christianity, nothing further need be remarked, except to call attention to its careful, finished style. One notable passage is the comparison between Plato's philosophy and Christianity. Augustine believed Plato himself would have supported Christianity if he had ever had a vision of its sublime magnitude and wide-reaching results in the world. Romanianus was evidently convinced, for soon thereafter he embraced the Christian faith.

When Augustine returned to his native town, it was with the sorrow of his mother's death still fresh in his breast. He was to take his departure with another grief pressing upon him. The boy Adeodatus had been with him constantly. In the studious atmosphere of the cloister he had developed marked mental qualities. His father was even alarmed at his precocity. There is left us an admirable book, entitled "The Master," containing a dialogue between the father, and his son, only sixteen. Augustine makes affidavit[11] that the arguments are all the lad's own. They lead up to the declaration of Christ: "One is your Master," and display considerable talent. But this "Gift of God," as his name, by strange inconsistency, signifies, was too frail to support so unusual a mind, and soon died. It was not long thereafter that the voices of a needy world called upon Augustine, with an urgency which the quiet of his seclusion would not allow him to escape.

---

[11] Confessions, IX, 14.

CHAPTER IX.

HIPPO REGIUS.

In the Church of Augustine's day, formalities were not always observed in the matter of selecting ministers. The story is well known of how Ambrose, an officer in the imperial service, was chosen bishop as the result of a child's crying his name in the Church, though he protested violently and had first to be baptized. A similar haste accompanied the choice of Cyprian as bishop of Carthage. It was in this way also that Augustine was dragged out of his retreat and thrust into the active service of the Church. In general, the Church was in a loosely-organized condition throughout North Africa. Ministers of thorough equipment were rare. Consequently Christian men of ability were eagerly watched. If a congregation spied out a promising person and summarily called him to a position, there was a prevalent opinion that he was bound to accept.[1] In the monasteries, especially, clerical recruits were sought. There is nothing surprising, then, in the discovery of the head of the convent at Thagaste. Indeed, so well and favorably known

---

[1] It is said that Synesius, whom Kingsley has made familiar, was made bishop in spite of his protest that he was both heretical and married.

did he become, that it was necessary for him to move about with the caution of "the hunted." He dreaded lofty position.[2]

But Augustine could not long avoid capture. One day he found himself urged by a State official, who had leanings towards the life of a recluse, to visit "Royal Hippo," a city on the coast. Whether this was a ruse or not Augustine did not consider, but set out on his mission of winning a possible disciple. The aged Valerius was at that time bishop of Hippo. When Augustine entered the Basilica of Peace—one finds it easy to imagine it all an adroit piece of stratagem—Valerius was insisting upon the necessity of the people's securing a new priest to aid him in his work. There was instant recognition of Augustine, and a loud cry for his ordination. They surrounded him and pressed him forward. In vain were protests and tears. There was no appeal. Such outbreaks were not uncommon in the early Church. In a letter to Jerome, Augustine relates the story of a certain bishop who got into trouble by quoting Jonah iv, 6, from Jerome's version. For generations the Church had chanted this passage. When, then, "ivy" was substituted for "gourd," such a tumult arose that the bishop narrowly escaped being left without a congregation.

The reluctance with which Augustine submitted to ordination was not due, as some conjectured from

---

[2] Sermon XLIX.

his weeping,[3] to the meagerness of his opportunity in Hippo, or to his being made presbyter instead of colleague of Valerius. As we have seen, he felt a natural shrinking from the burdens of the priesthood. He was thirty-seven years of age, and the bent of his life had been in a different direction. There seems to have been no other reason for his hesitation. Hippo itself was by no means an obscure place. Situated as it was on the seaboard, about two hundred miles from Carthage to the west, it had gained importance as a commercial outlet under the Romans. Some glory attached to it also as the former residence of the Numidian kings— whence the epithet "Royal." There were perhaps thirty-five thousand people there in Augustine's time.

Two rivers washed the walls of Hippo, the Sebus, and a smaller one to which the Arabs give the name *Abou-Gemma*. Various traces of Roman civilization are still to be found on the banks of these rivers. To the east stretched out the paths of the Great Sea. Back of the town arose the "Red Hill," decked with a fine array of fig, olive, and chestnut trees. On the southeast lay the yellow plains reaching out along the route to Carthage, as far as the bold promontory of the Atlas range, called now *Beni-Urgin*. In all, the town was about three miles in circumference. Within its inclosure, besides many gardens, were the basilica, baths, and

---

[3] See Ep. 21, and Possidius, C. 4.

a castle which served both as palace and fortress (being situated on a commanding hill in the middle of the town). There was a mixed population, and a very discordant one—disciples of Mani, Arians, Jews, Donatists, pagans in large numbers, and Catholic Christians. The last named, doubtless, were made up largely of handicraftsmen, fishermen, slaves, and gardeners. For forty years, Augustine was to labor among such people as these, gradually building up the Church from a humble place to one of power in North Africa. Nowadays, travelers often witness a strange sight among the ruins a mile from Bona. On Fridays a band of Mohammedans is likely to approach, burn a few grains of incense, sacrifice a bird, offer a prayer to "the great Christian" (Roumi Kebir), seeking his celestial favor, fire their guns, and depart. For even to-day the Arabs think of Augustine as a mighty friend of God.

Augustine did not take up his abode at Hippo immediately. Feeling his inefficiency, he first sought retirement and closer spiritual preparation. Presumably he returned for a brief time to Thagaste. There he made new-plans for the continuance of the little community. His closest friends did not forsake him, however. Near the church at Hippo was a garden, and this was given into his charge for the site of a new monastery. Alypius and Evodius, together with additional disciples, Possidius (who became the chief contemporary biographer of Augustine), Severus, and others, joined their leader in a life, as Possidius says, "according to the rule laid down by the holy apostles." Up to this time, there were few facilities for that special spiritual culture necessary in ministers of the Church. Hence the attainments of the clergy were often quite inadequate. The aim of Augustine was to provide candidates for the Church with mental and religious discipline. From his society went forth no less than ten bishops. After a while the monastery became so popular that others of a similar type had to be opened in Hippo. From the success of this one many other bishops were induced to found monasteries of the same kind, and a better trained clergy was the outcome.

Augustine's principal duty in his new surroundings was to preach. Bishop Valerius was of Greek extraction, and very feeble. Hence, he failed to meet the requirements of the place in two respects, —through his imperfect Latin and his weak body. It was an almost unprecedented performance for a humble priest to preach in the presence of a bishop. Jerome informs us that it looked very much as if the bishops envied the younger men, or would not deign to hear them. But the custom did not disturb Valerius. Protests came in from African bishops on all sides. He gave them no heed, but rather thanked God for sending him so gifted an assistant. It was not long before he had plenty of imitators, especially as his procedure was common in the East.

The preaching and monastic duties of Augustine did not prevent his engaging in literary labors, and withal in controversy. Christianity was being hard pressed in Hippo. The aged bishop, with his one Church, had found it a heavy problem to hold his own. With Augustine's coming we are told "the Church began to lift up its head." This was especially true with regard to the sect of Manichæans. Unquestionably they were the keenest and closest rivals Valerius had. But now they were to meet a worthier antagonist, one who had crossed swords with them before and was familiar with their tactics. Some time during the year of his ordination, he wrote the book, "On the Profit of Believing," directed to a friend who had become a Manichee chiefly through his influence. Apart from the autobiographical interest of the work, there is still pleasure in following Augustine's search for ultimate authority. Is it Scripture? or tradition? or the reason? or Christ? For answer, this advice is given: "Follow the pathway of Catholic teaching, which hath flowed down from Christ Himself through the apostles, even unto us." If you desire true religion, and dare first to believe you will attain unto it, and then yield your mind as a suppliant, you can not be disappointed. If you seek a more positive reason for following Christ, you must fall back upon "report strengthened by numbers, agreement, antiquity." Miracles and a multitude of followers are also held out as basis for belief. If Augustine had put together these loosely connected ideas, he might have reached a safe rule. But Augustine was never a profound systematizer. That he accomplished the practical result of recovering his friend Honoratus from error, was perhaps enough.

Not till the year following, however, did Augustine begin to display those gifts and graces which have led an eminent writer to describe him as "the most marvelous controversial phenomenon which the whole history of the Church from first to last presents."[4] There lived in Hippo a bishop of the Manichees, called Fortunatus. Up to this time he had held sway over the simple Hipponenses without a rival. All sects saw in him a dangerous foe. But, with the arrival of Augustine, fresh hope arose in the Christian camp. His distinguished abilities were relied upon to lay low the Manichæan's pride. Augustine was accordingly appealed to, and agreed to a public debate with Fortunatus. But he, in turn, showed less eagerness to display his reasons for the faith within him. He had depended less upon argument than upon rather loud-sounding pretensions. But the fight was on, and Fortunatus, being unable to escape, agreed upon a day and place for the contest.

Late in August of the year 392, at the baths of

---

[4] Canon Mozley, Ruling Ideas in Early Ages.

Sosius, a crowd of students, curious, and sectarians quickly gathered for the debate. Controversies of this kind were quite the vogue, and were as keenly relished by the audience as are the famous disputes on Glasgow Green in our own time. On the first day, it took Augustine very little time to force his antagonist to cover. Fortunatus had no liking for doctrine; he preferred to set up a vindication of Manichæan morals. (How modern!) In reply, Augustine certainly is less bitter in his denunciations. But it is because he would compel his opponent to keep close to their fundamental differences. The crowd were quick to appreciate. They saw that Fortunatus made short shift of Scripture, and was guilty of pitiable inconsistencies. At length they broke out into jeers and the meeting ended in clamorous confusion. Fortunatus departed from Hippo in shame to seek more convincing arguments from his superiors. Evidently he never found what he sought, for Hippo saw him no more. This was not the end of Augustine's campaign against the Manichæans. But he had dealt them an effective blow, and their further retreat in the West was due in very great measure to his unyielding assaults.

With the concluding scenes of this contest we are ushered into the beginnings of another. From his boyhood, Augustine must have known that the Church in Africa was rent by an internal strife. Of the origin and course of this schism we will speak more fully in a later chapter. The offending party, the Donatists, claimed to be the true Church. Thousands had grown up in that belief. In some places the sect outnumbered the Catholic Christians. Augustine, up to the year of his ordination, seems to have been little concerned. In the year 392, however, his eyes were opened. He chanced to be passing through a part of his bishop's see, when he came upon the labors of the Donatist Bishop Maximin. This man, though friendly to Christianity, was none the less zealous for his sect, and had rebaptized a Catholic deacon upon receiving him into the same office as a Donatist. This to Augustine was the central phase of the Donatist offense. In a letter to Maximin, whom, though he refuses to recognize his orders, he denotes *Dominus dulcissimus,* he expresses his confidence in his own notion of the Church, and in brotherly fashion invites Maximin to conference. Not content with this initial step, he resorted to a species of doggerel poetry—"A Psalm Against the Donatist Party." In the manner of the time this undignified utterance doubtless was to be sung in the streets. But it was probably too long for that purpose, and only the catching refrain, for peace and honest judgment, would attract popular notice. The principal arguments which Augustine was to employ with increasing ardor, if not bitterness, against the Donatists, are most of them found in this crude, unmeasured production. It was followed by a work no longer extant, designed as an answer to certain apologetics of Bishop Donatus, "the sphinx" of the sect.

In the year 393, an important council of all Africa was convened at Hippo. To Augustine was given the task of preaching the sermon. So far had he advanced in fame. He took for his subject, "Faith and the Creed," and such an impression did he make that he was induced to expand it into a larger treatise. The holy Catholic Church, he declared, had no place for heretics who differed in doctrine, or for schismatics, like the Donatists, who transgressed in the rupture of brotherly love. Augustine was influential in this conference in other ways. Probably it will remain best known by its relation to the formation of the New Testament canon, having settled for the first time upon the twenty-seven books to which we are still accustomed.

Among the practices of the Donatists were an encouragement of the martyr spirit and the attendant revelings at the tombs of dead heroes or in the churches. Unfortunately, the Catholic Church itself was not free from the abominations growing out of these customs. Almost every province and town had its martyr who held watch over its interests. In some cases, indeed, Christian martyrs were transformed into mythical beings of much the same type as the tutelary deities of the pagans. In order to compromise with the untutored converts from paganism, Christian bishops often had winked at the celebrations held in memory of the worthy dead. When charged with deifying the saints, teachers like Augustine and Chrysostom and Theodoret had to defend themselves by making it appear that the Church reverenced the martyrs only to recall their virtues. But it is certain that many abuses were connected with this veneration. It will be remembered how the simple-hearted Monica was forbidden the privilege of "feasting" in Milan, where the custom was suppressed. In Africa, many bishops gave their authority to these feasts, or *lætitiæ*. Augustine had written to Aurelius in 392 (Ep. 22), calling upon the Bishop of Carthage in most urgent terms to summon a council for the wiping out of these semi-heathen practices. The council of the following year accordingly decreed that the banquets should be discontinued "as far as possible."

This was too mild for Augustine. He considered the continuance of the superstitions deplorable, however popular. Rioting and drunkenness were every-day accompaniments of the services "designed to honor the memory of the blessed martyrs," and it was disgraceful that Africa should tolerate them longer. By 395, he was thoroughly aroused. Somewhat before Easter occurred the annual festival of Leontius, patron saint of Hippo. This anniversary was a signal for unusual indulgence on the part of both Donatist and Catholic. In a letter to Alypius (29), now become bishop of Thagaste, Augustine outlines his tactics. A few days before the festival, he preached concerning "dogs and swine,"—such they were who in riotous pleasure abused "the privileges which are the pearls of the Church." Few were present. But rumor of the sermon soon spread. Next day a great crowd assembled. Augustine spoke with all the passion of a reformer, his hearers and himself being melted to tears. Even then he had not completely carried the day; for, on the morning of the feast, there was still a disposition with some to devote themselves to excessive eating and drinking. With resolute purpose, he prepared one final denunciation, after which he was ready to "shake his garments and depart." "But then the Lord showed me that He leaves us not alone." The band of obstinates gathered in his presence, and listened to some earnest advice in response to their question: "Wherefore now prohibit this custom?" The remainder of the day was given over to worship and praise. As for the Donatist "brethren," no restraint was upon them. The noise of their Bacchic revels poured in upon the closing discourse of Augustine and he besought his humbled followers to recognize the deeper worth of things spiritual. This was the end of the feasts to the martyrs in the Church at Hippo, but the practice hung on in other parts of North Africa.

It was becoming dangerous for Augustine to venture far beyond the borders of Hippo. For one thing, the Donatists were resorting to violence.

They would unhesitatingly enter a church and tear down the altar.[5] The opposition of men like Augustine had made them firm and fierce. Catholics were assailed and terrorized. It was even boasted that the man would receive a rich spiritual reward who would make way with Augustine. On the other hand, the presbyter of Hippo was becoming widely known. His people feared to let him go a great distance from them, for the obvious reason that plenty of congregations, needing a bishop, would not scruple to lay under tribute his fine talents. Indeed, a deputation arrived at Hippo with suspicious designs, only to find the aged Valerius awake to his peril—Augustine was kept in hiding till their departure.

At last Valerius wrote to Carthage to secure the co-operation of Aurelius in elevating Augustine to the bishopric. Ecclesiastics from all directions came together. There was only one dissent, and that was by the bishop of Calamus, who alleged that Augustine had been charged with immoral conduct by the Donatists. The report was an absurd calumny, and Bishop Megalius afterwards sought Augustine's pardon. In fact, it was this same Megalius, who, in the absence of Aurelius, conferred upon Augustine the episcopal ordination, briefly before Christmas.

Augustine regarded the new office as a most responsible burden.[6] But it gave him larger scope

---
[5] See Augustine's Letter to Alypius, XXIX, 12.
[6] Ep. 31, 4.

for his tastes, both as ecclesiastic and controversialist. His senior bishop died shortly after, leaving him sole oversight of the "parish." Accordingly, he removed from the retired garden monastery to the former house of Valerius. It is here we next shall find him.

CHAPTER X.

THE BISHOP AT WORK.

To be a bishop, in the age of Augustine, was to be a successor of the apostles. The distinction between him and the presbyter was becoming more marked. Their primitive equal dignity was still maintained by Chrysostom, the golden-mouthed, and by Jerome. But the bishop was gradually entering into a place of patriarchal power. He alone could impart spiritual ordination, and confirm such as the presbyters had baptized, and grant absolution. In short, Augustine found himself raised to a much more representative position. But it meant to him additional turmoil and increasing ministerial labors.

Possidius, who for forty years lived in personal intimacy with the bishop of Hippo, has left no description of his appearance. What is known can be traced only to an uncertain tradition. We are sure of the plain frock, and the monkish hood drawn about his shaven head. And perhaps we can accept the long beard, "the wrinkles which deep meditation very early had made in his broad forehead," "the fire of genius tempered by an expression of kindness which lit up his eyes," "the harshness of his African figure," and the thin features, with all which later "biographies" have made us familiar. But there is greater interest in taking account of facts which we know. Together with Augustine in his episcopal residence were gathered such priests and deacons, similarly garbed, as were engaged in the labors of the parish. "All things in common" continued to be the law. No one could enter who did not renounce all property rights. So we find one of the priests, Leporius, hastening to sell all his goods and using them for charity. But this plan made room for the scandals of an occasional Ananias. In sermon 355, Augustine relates the case of a priest named Barnabas who saved enough while in the bishop's home to buy a piece of land. Another priest, Januarius by name, confessed on his deathbed of having laid by a comfortable sum of money, which he had pretended belonged to his daughter, a minor, who lived in a neighboring nunnery. When it was too late for any other use, he wished to leave the money as a legacy to the Church. Augustine very properly refused it.

Adopting Jerome's rule of a golden-mean for monks, Augustine is described as being neither overnice nor careless about his clothing, his bed, or his boots. His admiring flock proffered him garments of the costliest kind, but he refused to wear them. He publicly declared he would appear in nothing which would be unbecoming even to his humblest sub-deacon, and if they persisted in making such gifts, he would sell them in behalf of the poor. He was equally moderate at the table. Vegetables and herbs formed the bulk of the diet. Meat was reserved for the sick, or for such hospitalities as might be extended to strangers. Wine was permitted in small quantities. A passage in the "Confessions" (X. Ch. XXXI) can be interpreted to mean that Augustine was fearful of excesses in his eating and drinking. As early as 1689, accordingly, Pierre Petit advanced the notion that it was only the great bishop's strong mind which prevented his losing his balance under the influence of wine. But this is nothing more than rationalistic badinage. Augustine had not the robust constitution to indulge in hearty feasting. The old lung trouble reasserted itself in hemorrhoidal attacks; he was slight, thin-blooded, and highly sensitive; and what strength he had was worn down by endless toils and many fastings.

At Augustine's table, moreover, little levity was known. He preferred the seasoning of serious converse and spirited discussion, to which was added the reading of some religious work. The shadow of no scandal was ever permitted to fall upon the clerical group as they ate. A reminder of this rule was ever before them, engraved on the table: "This is not the place for carping critics." With Jerome, he had no quarter, for the man who spoke evil of another who was absent.[1] One day he was entertaining some neighboring bishops, who in the course

---

[1] See Jerome's Letter to Nepotianus.

of their conversation either forgot the rule or ignored it. Instantly Augustine was on his feet. With great warmth he declared the couplet should be effaced, or he must leave the table. But this was but a reflection of a broader sympathy with folks which made him friend to all oppressed. Much of his own simplicity of living was due to a desire that his resources might be available for all in need. "The glory of a bishop," it was his custom to say, "is his care of the poor." All the table ornaments and utensils were of wood or terra cotta, excepting the silver spoons. When the Church treasury was empty, and money was needed to restore captives and provide for the poor, Augustine had the sacred vessels of the Church broken and melted. It brought him reproach, but he appealed to similar conduct on the part of Ambrose, who said he had rather present Christ with souls than with gold.

Augustine had recourse to Ambrose also in the matter of rules for the priesthood. Among these was the advice that ministers should not constitute themselves match-makers, for fear they might expose themselves to the rage of disappointed husbands. Augustine himself went much farther. His priests must not make alliances for themselves. Indeed, so drastic was he in respect to women, that he visited only orphans and widows in trouble. No woman was permitted to dwell beneath his roof, not even his own pious sister and nieces. McCabe's curiosity is aroused as to what Jerome would have said of such practices. We are not left in doubt. In the famous letter to Nepotianus, the recluse of Bethlehem makes it perfectly clear that he was rigid in demanding uniform restraints upon the clergy. "Never or rarely," he wrote, "let the foot of a woman pass the door of your humble dwelling." Such caution doubtless was justified by the evils of the period. In one of his sermons, Augustine confessed he had nowhere found better men than in monasteries,—and he had nowhere found worse.

One is able to discover more trustfulness than discretion in Augustine's management of his business affairs. He is said never to have carried a key or a ring, since he neither received nor used gifts for himself. All revenues were intrusted to his clergy, and at the close of each year he heard a report of expenditures, but, with unquestioning simplicity, never had the reports audited. He was awakened to the danger of this system by the revelations of the fraud of Januarius. Upon closer inquiry, he found a deplorable condition. A majority of his priests and deacons, contrary to their vows, had slaves, or houses, or property. Augustine was slow to wrath. He appointed a period in which these entanglements of the world might be abandoned. When the time had elapsed, he announced to a thronging congregation that the offenders had decided to renounce all their possessions. This encouraged him to renew the solemn rule of poverty. "Let them appeal to a thousand councils against my judgment. Let them go beyond the seas, if they will, to bear their complaints against me. Whatever they do, if they remain not faithful to their vows, by God's help they shall not be received in this home, so long as I am bishop."[2]

It would have pleased Augustine better if the offerings of the faithful had been enough for his needs. But he was as usual dependent on the often unworthy rich, a condition which brought with it many problems. On the other hand, he was compelled from purely Christian motives to refuse bequests to which the law gave a clear title. Hence he warned parents to make no provision for the Church which would mean neglect of their children. It seems that a citizen of Carthage had made over all his property to the Church, having no expectation of children. But afterwards, when children appeared, the Bishop Aurelius gave back the whole: "For according to the civil law," says Augustine, "he might have kept it, but not according to the law of heaven."[3] Accordingly, Augustine was sometimes charged with taking little pains to endow the Church. A certain Bonifacius, of the guild of the navicularii, whose duty was to ship grain to Rome and other parts, made the Church at Hippo his beneficiary. In case of shipwreck, Bonifacius (or more likely the unfortunate crew, who would

---

[2] Sermon, 256.
[3] Sermon 356, 5. This sermon and No. 355 are called "On the Life and Customs of the Clergy," and afford many a curious glimpse of the habits of his community.

suffer torture for their testimony) must prove that the mishap was unavoidable, or make up the loss to the State. Augustine wisely refused to menace the Church with a judicial process, and even worse, by accepting the bequest. He was even more honorable, if not so worldly-wise, in rejecting gifts for the Church if they in any way injured the relations of the donor. Possidius declares he saw many such gifts declined. There is no evidence that Augustine ever had any lurking desires to follow the example of some bishops, and surround himself with an air of splendor. But his frugality did not lift him above suspicion. A priest named Honoratus had died, without will, in Thiave. Formerly he had been a monk at Thagaste. By civil law, this property should have gone to the man's natural heirs, but the Church at Thiave put in an urgent claim for the entire amount. Augustine and Alypius joined in resisting their demand, but agreed to give them one-half, the other half to be added to the resources of the establishment at Thagaste. One of Augustine's colleagues, Samsucius, was horrified at this transaction, which he considered unworthy of bishops. Therefore, Augustine in order to avoid all appearance of avarice or injustice, and to soothe the wounded feelings of the Thiavites, awarded them all the property. There is no difficulty in acquitting Augustine of any sordidness in the matter, but it is a valuable sidelight (or shadow) on the life of the Church in his day.

With his usual loyalty, M. Poujoulat defends Augustine's preoccupation with spiritual concern. The bishop of Hippo, he says, was interested chiefly in the higher things, and found it difficult to climb down from thoughts of eternity to listen to the noise of earth. This, of course, is a fair picture of the saint and of the proper halo, but it keeps us from getting near the man of busy interests that Augustine actually was. We find the world crowding in upon him with constant and varied distractions, and it improves our estimate of him. He had to turn his care not merely to clothing the poor, releasing the captive, guarding the financial interests of the Church, building a refuge for strangers, making arrangement for marriages, and a great variety of such minor matters, he also was looked to as a tower of help by oppressed and persecuted of all classes. By a gradual growth of the external authority of the Church, it came about that bishops obtained the right of moral supervision over judges and governors in their discharge of duties of State. In the name of religion they might intercede successfully even with emperors in behalf of "individuals, entire cities and provinces, who sighed under grievous burdens, laid on them by reckless, arbitrary caprice, or who trembled in fear of heavy punishments amidst civil disturbances." With such far-reaching privileges, there was, of course, room for abuses on the part of arrogant or obstinate ecclesiastics. A case in point is that of Macedonius, a judge who

The Bishop at Work. 129

writes to Augustine (Ep. 152) complaining of the occasional unreasonableness of intercessions, and denouncing bishops who whine when their haughty requests are denied. To prevent such perversions, a law was framed in 398, forbidding the clergy to aid undeserving criminals. Augustine himself put the right of intercession to frequent use. The humblest and the highest appealed to him for aid, and none were turned away without sympathy. Even pagans, if they had the temerity to expose their deities and themselves to Augustine's unflexible attacks, found his humanity always abounding. Fellow-bishops found him insistent upon "a square deal." Thus, when the aged Auxilus put a heavy ban upon a certain man of rank, and included all his household, Augustine protested with great vehemence, demanding to know wherein lay the justice of such a sentence. Elsewhere[4] we learn how orphans often were left to the protection of the bishop, and how the property of widows and orphans was left under his guardianship.

After the manner of the age, Augustine was also constituted judge many times. Often, indeed, it was in the episcopal court that he spent most of his time. Till dinner hour he would sit in judgment. Sometimes, even, he would fail to dine at all, but would pass the entire day hearing complaints and settling disputes. The decision of the bishop was legally binding according to a decree of

---
[4] Ep. 252 and Sermon 176.

Constantine. Thus an unusually heavy burden of a foreign nature was imposed upon the bishops. Late in his life, Augustine found it necessary, in order that he might give his attention to theological work, to relinquish this judicial business for five days each week. Even then they besieged him without mercy, till he was obliged to become severe in his demand for quiet. His reputation as an adjudicator spread throughout Africa. It must have been greatly to his distaste to be thrown into this constant, heated turmoil of men's contentions. Even a self-subduing saint is condoned for such a human complaint as Augustine finds it impossible to repress: "Depart from me, ye wicked men, for I would study the Word of God."[5] Of course there was much vexation aroused, whichever way he judged. But doubtless this was counterbalanced by the wide opportunity presented of getting near his people, and of urging upon them the blessedness of brethren dwelling together in unity.

But Augustine's chief function was to officiate each day at the celebration in the basilica. There was a simple liturgical service of psalms. The Lord's Supper was celebrated according to the genuinely Christian view "as representing the fellowship of divine life subsisting between believers, their Redeemer, and one another."[6] Above all,

---
[5] On the Psalms cxix, 115.
[6] Neander, II, 326. McCabe's remark, that the "mass was already a daily liturgical function in the African Churches," implies more than can be proved.

Augustine stood before his people in the rôle of preacher. It was not an uncommon thing for him to deliver two discourses a day, and preach five days in succession. There are in the Benedictine edition of his works, three hundred ninety-four sermons, of which thirty-one very likely are spurious. Besides these must be included many of the expositions of the Psalms. These were preached for the most part at Hippo, though he constantly found himself in demand at Carthage, at Constantine, at Calamus, at Cæsarea, and at every place he appeared throughout North Africa. This popularity was due in part to his growing reputation as the champion of orthodoxy, and in part also to his real oratorical genius. It is no heresy to say that all Augustine's sermons do not make lively reading. His audience was made up mostly of poor people, with slight education. And it must be said that the sermons have a simplicity which must have been peculiarly adapted to the intelligence of his hearers. From their effect, and such evidence as we have, we must judge also that they were given with commanding power and deep feeling. Augustine himself often wept as he spoke. "God alone knows," he said to his congregation, "with what trembling I stand in your presence to address you." One rarely discovers, however, any lack of boldness when he resorts to charges of vice, or perfidy, or delinquency on the part of his members. But undoubtedly he had in no small degree that grace of humility which is the foundation of the most noble preaching. Contrary to what we would expect from one of his training, he was less concerned for the ornaments of style than for direct appeal. He said that he cared not whether he pleased the rhetoricians, so long as the common people understood. No better example of his power, over the minds and hearts of his hearers, can be given than a scene which he himself describes.[7] At Cæsarea, in Mauritania, there occurred annually a violent upheaval of the entire town, a sort of faction-war, in which neighborhoods and homes were divided into bitter parties, and every one was bent upon killing as many others as possible. The clergy had made an unsuccessful campaign against this traditional custom, or *caterva,* as it was called. When Augustine visited the town, therefore, he was besought to use his talent against the horrible practice. "I strove with all the vehemence of speech that I could command to drive from their hearts an evil so cruel and inveterate." At length the congregation applauded, and Augustine felt they were being persuaded. But he continued with such fiery zeal that they burst into tears, and he knew he had possession of their hearts. He adds significantly: "It is now eight years or more since anything of the sort was attempted there."

Such successes were, however, only occasional. The people of the Hippo Church were pitifully jeal-

---

[7] On Christian Doctrine, IV, 24.

ous and unstable. They complained if their head pastor went away for a journey. Augustine must have suffered from the lack of appreciation, and from the misunderstandings, which every great personality has to face when crowded into cramping quarters. He was unable to carry his people with him into the rampant doctrinal contests of his day. So it is not strange that the sermons preached at Hippo begin in the first years with a show of careful preparation, but gradually descend into weakness and hurry of method. Often he came into his pulpit without having given his remarks previous thought. As he himself confesses, he would take his text from the passage read by the "prælector," and extemporize according to the impressions of the hour.[8] In the nature of the case, inspiration could not continue uniformly strong under such conditions. What Dr. Marcus Dods says of the writings of Augustine in general, applies with special force to the sermons—they "may be compared with his country, wide tracts of thin, sterile ground, interspersed with spots so fruitful as to be capable of sustaining the whole population and invite the weary to linger." As one winds his way through the ponderous six volumes of the Oxford translation of the "Expositions on the Psalms," it is to feel how provokingly predominant is the "thin, sterile ground." It may be said in extenuation, that allowance must be made for the prevalent allegorical

---

[8] On the Psalms, cxxxviii, 1.

method to which Augustine was bred. Or we may profit by the exhortation of Dr. A. Cleveland Coxe, and turn to Augustine if we wish "to catch the living spirit that animates the wheels of the Psalms." But, when all is said, and predispositions of reverence for patristics is laid aside, it must be admitted that the sermon-commentaries are rather solid than buoyant, ingenious than impressive, clever than winsome. For the most part, as a responsible critic has estimated, Augustine was an "expository lecturer,"[9] lapsing into many foolish and trivial blunders of exegesis, sometimes preaching from a text and sometimes not, resorting very little to illustration, though generally with telling effect. Although he was thus unequal, his sermons often have the swing of deep earnestness and mental power, and he must hold his place as the greatest of the Latin preachers.

One of the matters of particular interest, as indicating the daily occupation of Augustine, is his relation with eminent contemporaries. Antony, the father of monasticism, died two years after Augustine's birth. Athanasius, Gregory of Nazianzum, Basil and his brother Gregory, of Nyssa, and Ambrose, passed from the scene before the bishop of Hippo reached his day of power. The bishop of Milan seems not to have recognized the promise of the young rhetoric master. But Simplicianus, his successor in the Italian see, did not fail to show

---

[9] Edward C. Dargan, D. D., A History of Preaching.

Augustine the respect due one of his worth and influence. Another name of note in Augustine's age was Paulinus. This man was born of a senatorial house in Bordeaux, and himself attained to highest rank through his ability and culture. Contrary to his own wish he had been forced into the priesthood by the inhabitants of Barcelona, but had retired to Nola, where he added a sixth church of rare beauty to the five already built about the tomb of St. Felix.. In his letters to this devoted Christian, Augustine expressed himself with refreshing freedom and reality.[10] There ought to be mention, also, in passing, of the letters between Augustine and such representative men as Hilary, General Boniface, Aurelius, and Victorinus.

But of surpassing value are the relations between Augustine the greatest Churchman, and Jerome the greatest scholar, of that age. From the gloomy monastic cell of Bethlehem, Jerome had kept close to the world through a voluminous correspondence, learned writings on various phases of Old and New Testament scholarship, and controversies. Some of his work fell into the hands of Augustine, who at once set about to express in a letter his delight, and to lay before the famous recluse some of his own writings. This was in the year 395, while Augustine was still a priest. After begging Jerome to give the Christian students a Latin translation of the Greek Scriptures, he turned to criticise the

---

[10] See Eps. 24, 25, 30, 94, 121, 149, 186; also 31, 42, 45, 80, 95.

monk's commentary on Gal. ii, 11-14. This passage had been a kind of stumbling-block to some recent converts, and Jerome had made a bold assertion that Paul's withstanding Peter to the face was a preconcerted arrangement piously devised for its effect in a delicate situation. As a precedent in the interpretation of Scripture, this daring ingenuity hardly appealed to Augustine, and he frankly says so, though with proper courtesy. As this letter did not reach Bethlehem, Augustine made another attempt shortly after becoming bishop. By rare misfortune this letter also failed of its destination, and, by becoming a part of Augustine's other writings, reached Jerome by a long detour and after a wide reading in Rome and elsewhere. Not till the year 402 did Augustine hear through a traveler from the Holy Land, that in Bethlehem it was common gossip that Jerome had been attacked relentlessly by the new bishop of Hippo. He hastened to set the matter right in a kindly message to Jerome. But he was speedily to find that sainthood in the Eastern monastery was mixed with some spleen. The reply came at once, and, in spite of pretences of humility and love, showed that the old man's pride had been offended: "Far be it from me to presume to attack anything your grace has written. For it is enough for me to prove my own views without controverting what others hold. But it is well known to one of your wisdom, that every one is satisfied with his own opinion, and that it is puerile self-sufficiency to seek, as young men have of old been wont to do, to gain glory to one's own name by assailing men who have become renowned. Love one who loves you, and do not because you are young challenge a veteran in the field of Scripture."

Next year, by a young deacon on his way to the East, Augustine sent another letter. Perhaps he had not yet received Jerome's reply. At any rate, he resorts once more to a friendly criticism of some of his elder's work.

By this time affairs had become involved in a sorry tangle. The miscarriage of Augustine's letters, and their inclusion in his works as a kind of challenge to the old monk, could not be understood by Jerome. His natural pride, his dislike for opposition, his violent temper—all of which had broken forth in extravagant and scurrilous language upon his departure from Rome—had not been entirely repressed by the diligent labors and restraints of his ascetic retreat. He admits, in the letter of 403, a serious difficulty in regarding Augustine's explanation as guileless—a "honeyed sword" he calls it. The younger man's polite request that he should recall the ill-advised comment on Galatians, should "recant it in a humble Palinode," was a setting at naught of "the laws of brotherly love." "If you wish to exercise or display your learning, choose as your antagonists young, eloquent, and illustrious men, of whom it is said there are many at Rome." "You are challenging an old man, disturbing the peace of one who asks only to be allowed to be quiet." He adds rather snubbingly: "I can at this time pronounce nothing in your works to merit censure; for I have never read them with any attention."

In no passage of his history does the character of Augustine show to better advantage. Letters often were lost in the Roman world, when no government was responsible for their safe delivery. It ought not therefore to occasion surprise if the haughtiness, or blindness, of Jerome had at least ruffled the spirits of his critic. But Augustine hastened to show himself a man of peace. After freeing himself from Jerome's charge of insincerity and desire for self-exaltation, he concludes (Ep. 73): "If it be possible for us to discuss anything by which our hearts may be nourished without any bitterness of discord, I entreat you let us address ourselves to this. But if it is not possible for either of us to point out what he may judge to demand correction in the other's writings, without being suspected of envy and regarded as wounding friendship, let us, having regard to our spiritual life and health, leave such conference alone."

The response came in a long letter of eight thousand words. The rancor was still lingering in Jerome's breast. "I pass by," he begins, "the conciliatory phrases in your courteous salutation: I say nothing of the compliments by which you attempt to take the edge off your censure." He can not quite forget the smart of the imaginary "honeyed sword." As for the disputed Pauline passage, ought not the youthful bishop, his antagonist, to spread his opinions throughout the world, and thus engage all other bishops to adopt them? "As for me, in my forlorn monastery, with my fellow-monks, I dare not pronounce on such weighty questions, but rely chiefly on the interpretations of Origen and the other Greek theologians." This is both a sneer and a mistake. But it is not more unpardonable than the ungracious remarks about Augustine's deficiencies in Greek learning.

In another year, however, the cloud has passed. Jerome writes with pacified good-nature: "Let us quit quarreling. Let there be sincere brotherliness between us; and henceforth let us exchange letters, not of controversy, but of mutual charity. Let us exercise ourselves in the field of Scripture without wounding each other." It is hard to believe that Jerome, an old man of seventy-five, gave very minute care to Augustine's reply of ten thousand words, for he begs to be allowed the peace which an old veteran has earned. But in all the remaining letters there is a tone of friendliness, and even of admiration, on Jerome's part, while Augustine continues to respect and seek the opinion of the more erudite monk. Indeed, he forbore expressing himself on one subject until after Jerome's death in 419, lest by antagonizing the latter, he might sever the relations which grew in warmth till the last.

CHAPTER XI.

DONATUS.

It is now generally conceded by eminent scholars that what is known as Donatism did not originate immediately in a doctrinal dispute. Some French and German writers make large capital out of their theory of the growth of episcopal power and the popular uprising against it, as if this accounted for the famous schism. A closer scrutiny discloses the fact, that, while a point of principle soon cropped out, the controversy began with differences of a political and personal nature.

It is necessary to notice that the clergy did not all emerge from the Diocletian persecution (303-305) purged as by fire. In North Africa there had grown up a spirit of pride, fanaticism, and malice. All this came to view in a council of 305, assembled in the Numidian city Cirta, for the purpose of choosing a bishop for that place. The presiding bishop, Secundus, had certain grievances against Mensurius, head of the Church at Carthage. It appears that the recent persecution had found some of the bishops wanting in the true spirit of martyrdom. By force or by fear they had been induced to surrender to the pagan authorities the sacred writings. For this they were called *traditores*. It was assumed that if they had not thus saved themselves, they would have suffered violent death. On the other hand, there were many who courted martyrdom, imprisonment, and loss of goods, as things particularly pleasing to God and deserving the praise of men. Thus there arose two parties. The fanatical, superstitious party was led by Secundus, while Mensurius, seconded by his archdeacon, Cæcilian, opposed the imprudent veneration of men who had given themselves up to voluntary and unnecessary martyrdom. Upon opening the Council of Cirta, Secundus did not hesitate to lay bare his suspicions of the misconduct of his fellow-clergy. Some, he found, were falsely accused. Others, like Mensurius, had saved their lives by giving up other writings than the Bible. One Purpurius, a man of glowing temper, resented the inquisitorial spirit of Secundus, against whom he turned the probe by asking: "How did it happen you got off so easily, though it was known you had copies of the Bible?" Rather than subject his own conduct to such severe examination, Secundus accepted the advice of one of his colleagues to leave the whole matter to the judgment of God.[1]

---

[1] The transactions of this assembly may be followed in Augustine's work, Against Cresconius. The Donatists held, but on very insufficient ground, that the documents had been interpolated. Augustine himself had the advantage of coming to the controversy in the second or third generation. Optatus had written his History of Donatism in 374, and it is the classic on that subject. To Optatus, Augustine pays his respects in these words: "Optatus, of venerable memory, Bishop of Mileve in the Catholic Communion."

In the year 311, a date from which the Donatist schism must properly begin, Mensurius was summoned to the court at Rome to answer for the untamed ardor of an overzealous subordinate. Fearing, so it is alleged, that he might not return alive, he intrusted the hiding-place of the costly Church vessels to two of his clergy, Celestius and Botrus. Not content with this precaution he confided his secret also to a saintly woman of his congregation. As he had presaged, Mensurius died on his way home. Steps were taken at once for the election of his successor. Botrus and Celestius, it is still further alleged, having cast eyes on the wealth of the Carthaginian see, looked to the vacancy with covetous longings. Greatly to their chagrin, therefore, Cæcilian, the archdeacon, who had stood nearest the deceased bishop in his official duties, was chosen, and presently consecrated by Felix, Bishop of Aptunga. The wrath of the disappointed pair was not soothed by the next step. The aforementioned woman having testified as to the precious possessions of the Church at Carthage, Botrus and his confederate were obliged to bring forward the entire amount.

It is for these reasons that Optatus lays at the bottom of the Donatist division, "Greed and ambition." But those two words do not describe all the trouble. Cæcilian was out of favor with the party at Carthage that disputed the position of Mensurius; for it was while carrying out the bishop's policy that he had forbidden Christians to foster criminality by bearing food to the prisons for the relief of pseudo-martyrs. In this way he had run counter to the practices of a wealthy, and accordingly influential, Christian matron of Carthage, named Lucilla. This woman had obtained certain fragments of bones, which she pretended were relics of some martyr or other, and was in the habit of kissing them each morning previous to her partaking of the communion. The deacon Cæcilian concluded that such a silly superstition must be abolished, and roundly rebuked Lucilla. This humiliation she of course resented. And her resentment forms a third root of the Donatist controversy.

No sooner was Cæcilian elected and ordained than the combined and powerful forces of Lucilla, Secundus, Botrus, and Celestius set at work to oppose him. From Augustine,[2] we learn that the intriguers met in the house of Lucilla, (another instance in history of "dux femina facti.") They began by refusing to recognize Cæcilian as bishop. When challenged to bring forward their charges, they fell back upon the old North African principle that because Felix, the consecrating bishop, was a *traditor,* the ordination of Cæcilian was therefore invalid. Their insincerity in this position was at once manifest. Cæcilian (either from a desire for peace at any cost, or because he conceded the principle said to be at stake) offered to resign that he

[2] Sermon, No. 46.

might be consecrated anew by the bishops from Numidia. But they, in turn, after choosing a second bishop for Carthage, Marjorinus, a reader of the Church and a favorite of Lucilla, proceeded to excommunicate Cæcilian for submitting to unlawful ordination.[3] Thus was set adrift a division of the early Church, destined to a hapless, ugly career.

While Marjorinus took the nominal lead of the antagonizing party, the real head was at first Donatus, Bishop of Casæ Nigræ in Numidia. It was, however, another Donatus, successor of Marjorinus, in 315,[4] who gave the sect its name and was its soul. "And he was well suited to stand at the head of a party, being a man of fiery, untutored eloquence, of great firmness of principle, and of great energy of action." Under such leadership, the Donatists sought at the start the recognition of the Emperor Constantine. From Rome, Arles, and finally, Milan in 316, imperial decisions accordingly were given. But these were favorable to the Catholics, and frowned upon the Donatists. At length, wearying of their persistency, Constantine took from the offending party their churches and property, and otherwise persecuted them. His successors down to Valentinian and Gratian were less violent; but these last emperors adopted drastic

---

[3] It is gratuitous to say that this was done by the seventy Numidian bishops after "pocketing a heavy bribe from Lucilla," yet one of Augustine's critics goes that far, apparently for the sake of local color.

[4] At least this seems to me the true view of the matter. For conclusive reasons see Neander II, p. 190, f. n. 2.

and often ill-advised measures, which resulted rather in the spread of Donatism than in its suppression. During the usurpation of Gildo (an African prince who maintained himself as ruler of the African province after the death of Theodosius, till 398), the Donatists were shielded from imperial persecution, and gained steadily in power and numbers. In fact, there was no time during the entire century when their fierce spirit was subdued or their courage daunted. When Augustine confronted them at the close of Gildo's revolt, they were regarded as the national party, and outnumbered the Catholic Christians.

There is one phase of the controversy which forms a dark picture. In North Africa there lived a band of fanatical monks, who, despising work, wandered among the peasant huts, begging or exacting food and shelter. For this they were termed *Circumcellions* (men who wander among huts). They called themselves soldiers of Christ, and Christian Champions.[5] But their weapons were carnal. In claim, at least, they represented the puritanic spirit of that part of Africa. It was for this reason that they sympathized with the Donatist, or popular African, Church, which they pretended to protect. It was very easy to incite these people to any kind of wild outrage. Pretending to be fighters for God, they roved about the country seeking to arouse slaves against their masters, and

---

[5] Cf. Augustine, On the Psalms, cxxxii, 6.

debtors against their creditors. They compelled venerable heads of families to submit to degrading insults. They dragged rich Catholics from their chariots and then harnessed them in place of the horses. They showed merciless disrespect to the Cæcilianist bishops and presbyters, and shamefully desecrated their churches. Indeed, they shrank neither from the destruction of churches nor from the murder of those who resisted them. When they themselves found opportunity, they "rushed headlong into the joy and crown of martyrdom," throwing themselves over precipices, leaping into fires, and paying others to kill them.[6]

By far the most important phase of the Donatist schism is Augustine's connection with it. When he came to Hippo, the Donatists were greatly in the majority, and he informs us that so strained were the relations, that in a time of stress no Donatist would venture to bake bread for a Catholic.[7] By this time, also, numbers were not the only formidable asset of the Donatists. They had had nearly a century in which to organize themselves into a compact body, and they stood for very definite and vigorous principles. Among these the most pronounced were an insistence upon a holy membership of the Church (the true Church consisting only of such as were known or thought to

---

[6] For confirmation of these statements, and for details, see Augustine's Letter to Count Boniface, No. 185, and the account in Optatus, Chaps. II and III. Augustine, in Ep. 35, tells of the insolence shown him by one of the Circumcellions.   [7] Against the Letters of Petilianus, II, 184.

be faithful); the rebaptism of *traditores;* the absolute separation of Church and State; the invalidity of baptism and ordination conferred by ecclesiastics of doubtful character. Had these adversaries, of what was prevalently known as Cæcilianism, been consistent, or able to maintain their positions, they might have wrought permanent disaster to the Catholic Church. But with such unwearied zeal did Augustine take up and continue his warfare, that long before the close of his life there was a complete reversal of the standing of the two parties.

We have already had occasion to speak of Augustine's engagements with the Donatists in the early years of his presbyterate at Hippo. Up to the year 398 nothing further occurred of enough interest to claim our attention. In that year, Honorius replaced the defeated Gildo. This meant a renewal of the oppressive laws of Theodosius, and a check upon the Circumcellions. But the imperial restraints were not at this time Augustine's chief reliance. He continued to make the most of letters, sermons, public debates, and controversial writings. No opportunity escaped him.[8]

Very little is gained by undertaking a minute examination of all Augustine's work in antagonism to the Donatist position. But it is important to glimpse the principal facts.[9] One of the most able disputants on the other side was Parmenian, suc-

---
[8] See Ep. 44, written in 398.
[9] A fuller account may be found in Dr. Hartranft's Introduction Essay to the Anti-Donatist Writings, Post Nicene Fathers, Vol. IV.

cessor of Donatus in Carthage. In defense of his party, he held that the Donatist communion was without blemish, and that it was essential to separate the evil from the Church in order to preserve the true notion of the Church inviolate. But in arriving at this end, the interference of the State must be deprecated. In reply Augustine defends the use of secular power, but charges the Donatists with originating the custom of appeal thereto. With many thrusts, he shows how impossible it has been for the Donatists themselves to maintain a pure membership or a blameless ministry. Yet he confesses the need of discipline. Appealing to Cyprian, he emphasizes the need for unity, and the sin of schism, in the Church, and makes much of the note of universality, the true Church being diffused throughout the whole world. All this has a particular bearing on Augustine's later attitude.

It was not, however, till later in the same year (400) that he set himself to elaborate a treatise against the Donatists, "On Baptism," and one in refutation of the contentions of Petilian, Donatist Bishop of Constantia.[10] In the latter of these, which is in three books, one finds a great deal of sterile and intemperate speech in place of argument. Augustine charges his opponent with "foolish loquacity" and "impious pride," derides his "panting lungs and swollen throat," and in closing makes a modest comparison between his own claims

---

[10] Against the Letters to Petilian.

and those of Petilian. The third book, indeed, can hardly be dignified by the term "argument:" it is at best only verbose and often unsuccessful rebuttal of rather lame propositions, mixed with liberal lumps of self-vindication. In book two, Petilian presses for an answer to the questions: "What have you to do with the kings of this world?" "If you wish us to be your friends, why do you drag us to you against our will?" The first question, Augustine turns back upon the Donatists—Why did they consort so closely with the apostate Julian?[11] As to the second query, Augustine makes a firm denial of any intention to coerce. It was not against their will, he said; for they were like children who needed to learn freedom through restraint and compulsion: "The very object of our negotiations with you is that you should cease to be heretics, and when you come over from your heresy to us, you cease to be what we hate, and begin to be what we love." In all this it is seen how Augustine gradually became hardened in the conflict. He began with intense disbelief in the employment of force, expecting by impassioned argument to win over his enemies. But he found the evil deep-seated and his foe stubborn. At length he was glad to look to a stronger arm for co-operation.

It is in the other work, "On Baptism," that we

---

[11] Under him the Donatist party received new life, their exiled bishops were recalled, and they were given back their property and rights of worship. Of course, these facts could not justify Augustine in his defense of the use of imperial force. The comparison was ill-drawn.

come more directly in contact with the core of the dispute. And here, Cyprian, as Professor Harnack has expressed it, "was played off against himself." It is chiefly around this bishop-martyr, therefore, that the discussion ought to be studied. Augustine held to the necessity of baptism to salvation, but considered it of value only when accompanied by regeneration. In any case, the character of the administrator was a matter of indifference, as long as Christ's institution was followed. If, therefore, the ordinance was administered in an heretical sect, it was a real baptism; but inasmuch as under such conditions, there could be no spiritual power of a new life, the ordinance was ineffectual. For, holding as he did, the unity of the Church, it was impossible in Augustine's mind for a man to find salvation outside the Catholic communion. This was the essential position of Cyprian. The man who leaves the Church sins against love and humility. And that was a precise description of the Donatist. When he returns to the Catholic unity, it is to receive the spirit signified by the rite already bestowed; for now he has healthfully what he previously had hurtfully and unworthily.[12]

On their side, the Donatists contended they were the true Church. Going back to the source of the schism, they declared that, since the ordination of Cæcilian by Felix was the act of a *traditor,* the party of Augustine, which descended from Felix

---
[12] On Baptism, VII, 41.

and Cæcilian, could by no means be the Church. Moreover, the Church, in order to be true, must cast out such as are of impure life, both lay and cleric. If men were baptized by a faithless minister, it was not faith they received, but guilt. Hence they must be rebaptized. To support this claim, reference was made to Cyprian, and the Carthaginian Council of 265. Thus it is seen how the authority of Cyprian was made to stand, on one hand for the preservation of unity, and on the other, for the repetition of baptism.

But, to get back to the current of events. While Augustine was busy with tongue and pen, and gradually was breaking away from these more peaceful measures to place reliance on State interference, the *Circumcellions* were becoming more active. But the struggle was beginning to count in favor of the Catholic Church. Many Donatists came over to Augustine's view, and, according to a decree of 401, passed in the Council of Carthage, these recedents received liberal treatment. At another general council, of 403, measures were adopted looking to a friendly discussion of contested points. Thus encouraged, by what looked like favorable progress, Augustine addressed a general letter (No. 76) to the Donatists, calling upon them not to imperil their salvation by persisting in disunion, and exposing their inconsistencies. This had an opposite effect to what he intended. Instead of being won to an attitude of open-mindedness, the Donatist bishops were highly incensed, and their allies, the easily-inflamed Circumcellions, committed fresh indignities. At a council held in Carthage the next year (404), accordingly, the prominent question was, whether new penal laws should not be sought against the Donatists. Augustine took the position that compelling men to belong to the Catholic body was only to make hypocrites. The truth must be its own defense. But he did not carry the council entirely with him. Indeed, it was not long before the Donatists found themselves the objects of a merciless attack at the hands of the Emperor Honorius. As heretics they were deprived of property and the right to receive legacies; many were heavily fined, and in Carthage, the sect speedily dropped out of view.

This activity of Honorius was regarded as commendable by the majority of Catholics. Augustine himself seems by this time to have suffered a complete change of heart. He had preferred moral force, but it had not won the day. Although the Donatists of better disposition disclaimed responsibility for the fury of the Circumcellions, we have Augustine's word that Catholics could not possibly have lived in the country were it not that city Donatists were held as hostages for their protection. In a letter to Vincentius (No. 93), he defends his sympathy for the use of civil constraints. "The important point," he says, "it not whether a man is coerced, but to what he is coerced." Justification for imperial decrees is found in their good results. Many a Donatist has lived to be grateful that unusual pressure led him to see more clearly the Catholic position. Religious coercion is like the force by which a sick man is kept from hurling himself from a window. It is strange to find Augustine in the same breath, with all this, appealing to the tolerance of Cyprian. In fact, one has little difficulty in spying out broad inconsistencies between the views of 398 and those of 408. In this instance it must be acknowledged that principles, with Augustine, changed with exigencies. Success was his vindication.

During the next few years, Augustine wrote several important letters,[13] and sermons in antagonism to the Donatists and in explanation of his own convictions. There is also a careful work entitled "Against Cresconius," in which he goes over the old questions concerning baptism, persecution, ordination and unity. Of the letters, the ones to claim our particular attention relate to political events of deep significance. In the year 408, Stilicho, to whom Theodosius had entrusted his two sons, Arcadius and Honorius, and who was the real ruling power of the West, was cruelly assassinated. The man who succeeded him, as *magister officiorum*, Olympius, found North Africa in commotion on account of religious strife. He sought the counsel of Augustine, who, in return, points to the practical

---

[13] See especially Nos. 86, 87, 88, 89, 97, 100, 105, 106, 108, 111, and 112.

benefits of coercion, and begs him await the return of an episcopal commission, which was even then on its way to Italy, in search of imperial aid against the mad unrestraint of the Circumcellions. The commission did its work well. It was not long before the forces of government were working smoothly, beside the earnest arguments of Augustine, to bring reluctant Donatists into the Catholic fold. Meanwhile, the storms were gathering about the hills of Rome. It would not do for the emperor's forces to be divided in Africa, upon the possession of which the Goths now looked with envious eyes, for there was the granary of Rome. In consequence, Honorius sent to Africa this short decree, intended to crush out as quickly as possible, the formidable army of Circumcellions: "Let them suffer by proscription and death if they dare to meet again in criminal audacity." This was followed within a few weeks, by another decree, intended to bring about a quiet ending of the differences between Donatist and Catholic. According to this plan, there should be a Conference at Carthage, at which representatives of both parties should argue their cases in the presence of a civil judge. This was in accord with a wish which Augustine and his fellow-bishops long had sought to bring to fulfillment.

In October of 410, edicts concerning the conference were sent out by Marcellinus, the tribune. It was not, however, till the following May that the same officer convoked the assembly and proceeded to sit in judgment over it. There were in all five hundred and sixty-five bishops, of whom a trifle more than half were Catholic. This is a smaller body than a Quadrennial Conference of the Methodist Episcopal Church. But there were no committees to arrange every detail and discussion. "The business," exclaimed Bishop Petilian petulantly, "belongs to those who concocted this whole affair." Hence it was nobody's business. The Donatists from the start were suspicious, and the transactions were noisy and disorderly. Whether it displayed any magnanimity or not, the Catholic bishops set out with a proposition that if the Donatists lost their cause they would share their own parishes with them, but if the Catholic cause were defeated they would yield their Churches to the Donatists. Perhaps the result seemed like a foregone conclusion anyway. Marcellinus was a devoted Catholic.

Augustine, in a sermon previous to the conference, had counseled love and gentleness. But his exhortation bore little fruit. The first day was consumed in a tiresome wrangle over questions of privilege, and the second day in an even more monotonous debate on delay and adjournment. For the Donatists, the chief speaker was Petilian, and on the other side, Augustine. Marcellinus invited all the bishops to be seated as he himself was. Only the Catholics complied. Petilian, on behalf of his colleagues, declared they could not sit down with such adversaries. Thereupon the imperial commissioner ordered his own chair removed and he and his officials remained standing. With undisguised malice, Petilian renewed the old trumped-up charges that were made against his great rival at ordination, but the matter was ruled out. When the unwieldy body finally settled down to the points at issue, there was a spirited and long-continued discussion. The pronounced differences were not long in coming to view. There was first of all the historical question, as to the origin of the schism. Was Cæcilian validly consecrated? Or was Felix lawfully qualified to consecrate? Both were denied by the Donatists. For his side, Augustine declared the allegations of his opponents totally groundless.[14] But even if Felix was a *traditor,* his act had the sanction of the Church and was therefore lifted beyond question.

Although the doctrinal issues did not all come to the front in the Council of Carthage, there were certain great questions involved, which summarize the controversy, and must receive brief treatment. First of all, *What is the Church, and who belong to it?* On the Donatist side, it was declared that the Church is what you see, provided priests are "pure" (neither heretics, *traditores,* nor otherwise unworthy) and members are holy and validly baptized. The counter-proposition of Augustine was that wheat and tares must grow together, after the parable of Christ, the true Church being the Catholic which

---

[14] Repeated research has borne out this contention of the Catholic party. See Hurst, History of the Christian Church, Vol. I, p. 251, f. n. 2.

is visible in the sacraments.[15] The second question had to do with *the validity of ordination and the sacrament of baptism.* As already noted, the Donatist contention was, that only priests of spotless character could duly administer these sacraments; this accounted for their practice of rebaptism. According to Augustine, on the other hand, the sacrament of baptism was independent of human disposition. It possessed a sort of magical efficacy which depended, not on any human factor, but upon "the Word and sign."[16] If bestowed by heretics, it was still valid, and became "efficacious unto salvation" upon the wanderer's returning penitently to the Church. While it is true that the Donatists were not consistent on this question in practice, it is equally true that Augustine could not be consistent in his defense of the position he took. For one thing, it ran counter to his thesis that the sacraments belong inseparably to the Catholic Church. Moreover, it was a denial of his view of the supreme authority of the Church. This raised a third question as to *"the seat of authority."* The Donatists appealed to visions, miracles, the hearing of prayer, the holiness of their bishops. These were satisfactory evidence of the truth and worth of their Church. But the Catholic Church, said Augustine, admitted no testimony but that of God in the Holy Scriptures. All other evidence

---

[15] This question will receive further attention in the next chapter.
[16] See Ep. 173, 3, On Baptism, IV, 6, 16; VI, 1.

was without validity. Because the Catholics had this Scriptural witness, they constituted the sole true Church. But, in the next place, *what are the true notes of the Church?* "Holiness," said the Donatists. "Yes," was the reply, "but only in a limited sense; namely, in that the Church, while necessarily made up of good and evil, must employ discipline; and also, because the Church in its sacraments, and in its union with Christ, has the only efficient means of sanctification." Other important marks of the true Church, according to Augustine, were unity, especially in faith and love; universality —*i. e.,* "identical with itself" everywhere and always;[17] apostolicity—possession of the apostolic writings, and unity based upon episcopal succession down from the apostles. In all these respects, it was claimed, the Donatists were lacking, and could not, therefore, be the true Church.[18] But, finally, *how far is physical force admissible in matters of religion?* The Donatists denied that the Catholic Church "had a divine right to rule the conscience." It may be they went too far in their setting forth of the opposition existing between Church and State. But their fundamental assertion was most defensible—that "the peace of Christ," in the words of their Bishop Gaudentius, "never forces men against their wills." In oppos-

---

[17] See the statement by Prof. Rainy, The **Ancient Catholic Church,** p. 418, f. n. 1, on p. 419.

[18] Cf. Harnack, V, pp. 144-155.

ing this principle, Augustine doubtless was caught in the subtle toils of the time-spirit. The age was with him in yielding to imperial power the settlement of religious disputes. And too easily did he go over to the side of those who misapplied the words of Christ—"Compel them to come in." Thus he gave his weighty influence to a theory which "contained the germ of that whole system of spiritual despotism, of intolerance and persecution, which ended in the tribunals of the Inquisition."[19]

It is clear that the results of the conference of 411 were not satisfactory to the Donatists. Marcellinus, as was expected, gave his decision in favor of the Catholic party. To them the Donatists were bidden turn over all their churches, while they themselves were prohibited from holding services any longer. This outcome only incensed the weaker side. Talk of unfairness and fraud was rife. A law of 414 was added, by which Honorius sought to crush the Donatists beyond all hope of reawakening. This naturally aroused furious indignation among the Donatist body. But they were weakening, in fact, becoming helpless. They now began to display a reckless indifference to life. Augustine describes (Ep. 172) one who threw himself violently from a horse, and another who plunged into a well. Of their savage, desperate conduct at this time we have vivid pictures in the letter to Boni-

---

[19] Neander, History of the Christian Religion and Church, Vol. II, p. 217. Cf. Allen, Continuity of Christian Thought, p. 153.

face, afterwards issued as a separate work under the title "On the Correction of Donatists."

In the year 418, Augustine joined in a conference at Cæsarea, at which Emeritus, Donatist bishop of the city, was present. As he was considered the best of the seven Donatist disputants at the Council of Carthage,[20] Augustine invited him to defend his position, but he sullenly held his peace, except to say that his party were not defeated by the truth so much as oppressed by power. The renewal, in this same year, of the obnoxious edicts, was followed on the one hand by many suicides and murders, and on the other, by many "conversions." Thus the conflict continued, so far as Augustine was interested, down to within a few years of his death. When the Arian Vandals devastated Africa, Catholic and Donatist suffered alike. Traces of this unusually persistent and daring sect are found (chiefly through the letters of Gregory the Great) down to the sixth century. Every effort to identify them with the modern Baptists has proved of little value. With all their inconsistencies they stood for certain high principles, such as the separation of State and Church, and the necessity for a Church "holy and without blemish," which, if they had prevailed, would have saved the Church both shame and humiliation.

---

[20] See Ep. 87.

CHAPTER XII.

THE TWO CITIES.

It is of deep significance that the writing of Augustine's "City of God" was coincident with the collapse of paganism and the fall of Rome. To understand this great book, one must begin with an examination of what was going on in the "city of men."

Some chapters back, I tried to make it plain that the old religion of the empire received a decisive setback under the young Valentinian in 384, the year Augustine was sojourning in Rome. From that time the dissolution of paganism was rapid and certain. Especially in the East, under repressive measures, pagan worship had a hard fight for life. At Alexandria, the colossal statue and temple of Serapis were destroyed, and all other temples were either brought low or turned into churches. The offering of sacrifices became a crime of high treason, punishable by death. If Arcadius, the youthful son and successor of Theodosius in the East, moved more cautiously for the sake of political advantages, his hesitation was quickly overcome by the crafty empress, Eudoxia, who sought merit for herself by her zeal in destroying idolatrous temples.

History was making rapidly in the western part of the empire. Symmachus and his party found the collusion between Rome and Milan too cogent a force for their progress. For in 391, Valentinian II was led to issue an edict closing the doors of the temples and putting a restraint upon heathen sacrifices. Then, to be sure, with the murder of Valentinian the very next year, there dawned a temporary hope for the pagans. A rhetorician, Eugenius, through the influence of the pagan general, Arbogast, took the reins of government. Against those pagan influences to which Eugenius owed his position, the voice of Ambrose now had little weight. The statue of Victory was restored to the forum. The antagonistic laws of former emperors were annulled. For two years careless Rome reveled again in the rites and sacrifices connected with her gods. But the Emperor Theodosius had only gone "on a journey." In 394 he returned. With a powerful army he crushed the forces of the usurping Eugenius, and, entering the city, began to put the Christian religion on its feet again. That his efforts were not fruitless, may be gathered from a letter of Jerome's, written a decade later, in which he describes the Roman temples as covered over with dirt and other signs of neglect.

This act of Theodosius was most timely. In another year he was dead. Honorius, to whom he left the government of the West, reiterated the laws of his father, but could not back them with the same stable power. The inconsistencies of treacherous governors, and the almost uninterrupted political turmoil of the period, made the re-enactment of the laws a continual necessity. In the provinces, especially, there were difficulties attending the suppression of paganism, and Africa had its share. The year 398 seems to have been a year of expectation and unusual energy among adherents of the expiring cult. An unknown wag had gotten up some Greek verses which purported to be the utterance of a sacred oracle. These declared that Peter, by magic arts, had brought it to pass that the religion of Christ should have a duration of 365 years, beginning with the year 33, on the Ides of May—the day of the sending of the Holy Spirit. It was then to come to a sudden end.[1] This may account in part for the rejuvenation of paganism in this fateful year. And this reawakening is sufficient in itself to account for the restrictive measures of 398 and 399. It is gratuitous to force upon Augustine responsibility for the temple-destroying passion which in these years seized the imperial power.[2] One characteristic incident was the attempt of a heathen magistrate to gild the

---

[1] This matter is discussed by Augustine in the City of God (XVIII, 53 and 54), where he heaps fine scorn upon those who trusted in the reputed "oracle."

[2] For an example of strained logic, in this connection, see McCabe (p. 334), who claims to be "compelled to conclude that Augustine and the Carthaginian bishops started the persecution of the old religion in Africa."

beard of a statue of Hercules in Carthage, and the consequent horror of the Christian part of the populace. Encouraged by Augustine, it may be (for he chanced to be preaching in Carthage at the time), they demanded that idols should be torn down in Carthage as they were in Rome. Moreover, there was unusual indifference to the laws among pagan landholders. With great difficulty, Augustine preserved to the Church peasants under such temptations to indulge in heathen worship. In other cases, he was obliged to restrain his people from demolishing idols upon neighboring estates. Accordingly Honorius gave new sanction to former edicts, by ordering the destruction of all heathen places of worship in the country. It is certain, however, that the execution of this order extended also to the cities; for we have Augustine's word that in 399 two officers of Honorius, Gaudentius and Jovius, entered Carthage and overthrew all temples and images.

All this, of course, brought pagan and Christian factions into embittered relations. Acts of violence became frequent. In Suffectum, a town of Tunis, a bloody riot resulted from the demolition of a favorite statue of Hercules. When the tumult had quieted, it was found that sixty Christians had been killed. Blame for the outrage was put upon the magistrates of the town, and they seem to have appealed to Augustine for an adjustment of difficulties, and especially for restoration of the lamented

Hercules. In his reply (Ep. 50), Augustine charges them with flagrant disrespect of imperial authority, and scornfully offers to make good the loss of their god. "Fear not, your god is in the hands of his makers, and shall be with all diligence hewn out and polished and ornamented. We will give in addition some red ochre to make him blush in such a way as may well harmonize with your devotions." His only condition is that they restore, on their side, the lives of the sixty martyrs.

A different light is thrown upon the declining pagan worship by another letter (232), in which Augustine takes exception to the manner in which the citizens of Madaura had addressed him as "Father," while wishing him "health and a long life in Jesus Christ the Lord." He notes that Madaura has suffered no change of heart since his student days there, and therefore regards their salutation as mockery. Though he looks upon them as "fathers," yet he abhors their idolatrous worship and points them to Christ. Such opportunities of drawing a Christian lesson he never let pass. Thus he was able to exercise a most wholesome influence over pagans of nobler mind, such as Dioscorus, the emperor's remembrancer, and Longinianus, a learned grammarian of Madaura.[3]

Meanwhile affairs were hurrying to a crisis in the once imperial city. Stilicho, the daring Vandal, who had been the directing genius of the empire,

---

[3] See Letters 117 and 118, 133, 134, and 135.

came under the suspicion of Honorius, who caused his death. This act precipitated a fresh attack upon Rome by the barbarians under Alaric, whom Honorius hitherto had succeeded in buying off. The haughty leader of the Gothic forces was reminded of the immense population of the city, but replied laconically: "If the hay is thick, the easier will be the mowing." Once more, however, Honorius proffered a heavy ransom, and for a time the city was at ease again. But a new pretext soon brought Alaric to the gates. By seizing Ostia, he was enabled to make demands upon the senate. As a result, Attalus, a Greek Arian and prefect of the city, was appointed puppet emperor. Rome now rejoiced in a renaissance of religiosity of the Olympian mold. Honorius was reduced to desperate straits in his capital stronghold, Ravenna. About to yield, two things saved him. First, enough cohorts arrived to make his own position impregnable. Then, in Africa, whose possession was indispensable to Rome, Heraclian, true to his emperor, easily disposed of the meager troops sent by Attalus to depose him. In anger, the dreaded Alaric moved upon the fated city. Slaves within made an entrance possible. Attalus was deposed. On the twenty-fourth of August the pillaging of the city began. For six frightful days the destructive work went on, only Christian buildings being spared. Heathenism was receiving a mortal blow at its life-center. With weakening pulse-beat the ugly body was tottering to doom. A few devotees there continued to be for another decade. But when Theodosius II decreed, in 423, that confiscation of property, and banishment, should be the fate of any remaining pagans, he was constrained to add: "That is, such pagans as survive, although we believe there are none."

For Christianity, also, there was a severe shock in the fall of Rome. A tremor ran through the empire. Men were not only alarmed; they were filled with awe and wonder. They must find a cause for the awful disaster. And, to the pagan mind, the only adequate explanation was the supernatural one—the gods of Rome had been outraged; their altars deserted; their temples closed. For a millennium these ancient deities had defended the city, and given her unprecedented power. At length, amid the frittering away of their worship, their patience was exhausted, and it was they who had visited calamity upon the empire. The corollary to all this proved a severe tax upon the faith of multitudes of Christians. They were the responsible party, for they had led men to accept their God under pretense that universal peace and bliss would follow. Thus Christianity came to be confronted with a new and twofold peril, that from within, and another from without. Especially was the cry widespread and bitter from without. Christian preachers found themselves called upon to employ all their resources in defense of the faith. "The gods," said the sullen pagan, "have struck us down for our faithlessness, and the Christians must bear the blame."

We may pause long enough to see that such a charge was unsupported, although Gibbon and some other secular historians sympathize with the pagans in their complaint. As Christian apologists everywhere, and none so stoutly as Augustine, protested, it was just the forces arrayed against Christianity that had caused Rome's downfall. A disinterested judgment must pronounce the difficulty to have been an unchecked, inner disease. Indeed it is quite impossible to understand how Christianity was at all accountable. What had the Christian religion to do with that "vast, dimly-known chaos of numberless barbarous tongues and savage races," which stretched northward and northeast of the Roman borders, and as early as the days of the first Cæsar began that restless crowding down the Danube, which at length was to bring them to the walls of the "eternal" city? Or how could Christianity be called to account for the soddenness of the people of the empire, the avarice of petty governors, the stupid treatment of the alien races, the effeminacy and recklessness of the "nobility," the repetition of wasteful and needless wars, or for the spiritual deadness and rank unconcern of men and women submerged in doltish dissipation?[4] As for the emperors who bore the name Christian, one is

---

[4] Cf. Augustine in a letter to Marcellinus, A D. 412. He is speaking of the age of Cicero. See Ep. 138, Chap. III.

perplexed to know how the empire could have been better protected had they been pagan. The fact that several of them were mere boys, and most of them incapable, is by no means chargeable on their religion. There is this much true, however, that the Christian clergy of the age were often perfidious, or devoid of a high sense of their responsibilities. In the message which the Great Apostle preached to the end, in the Roman capital—"the Kingdom of God," and "the things concerning the Lord Jesus Christ"[5]—was the only hope of the kingdom of men. Had that message continued to be preached, in singleness of purpose and sincerity of heart, and reasonably heeded by Rome's poor and her mighty, the page of history would wear a far more attractive aspect.[6]

Among the wealthy inhabitants of Italy, who poured into North Africa during and after the terrible siege, was the noble widow of Sextus Petronius, once prefect and most noteworthy citizen of Rome. Proba had given three sons to the service of the empire (in the consulship), and, in her splendid palace had maintained one of the chief centers of Christian influence in the city. Accompanied by her daughter-in-law, Juliana, and her granddaughter, Demetrias, she put off in a small

---

[5] Acts xxviii, 31.
[6] The group of letters, Nos. 132–142, is of great interest, and will repay a careful reading. Whatever may be said of the discontent with Christianity, "which rolled sullenly through the provinces," there are tokens in these letters that much of the best thought of the time was directed towards Christianity for help.

skiff from which they watched the burning of their luxurious home. Landing at Carthage with such fragments of their vast fortune as they had been able to save, a worse fate was hardly averted. The Count Heraclian, having preserved Africa to Honorius was apparently seized with personal ambitions of wide-sweeping proportions. With a strong hand he was master of the African situation, while the emperor was hopelessly weak and his empire in a state of hastening ruin. It was an hour of destiny for a man of vision and action. But Heraclian was not long in proving he was not that man. With the flight of so many families of rank to his asylum, he was smitten with a blinding greed for gold. Female fugitives were confronted by his accomplices at the port of Carthage, and compelled to pay dearly for protection from the ravishments of the Goth, or the oppression of the slave-dealer. It is charged that Heraclian demanded large sums from helpless maidens of noble birth, and, when they could not pay, sold them to Syrian merchants, to be disposed of in Oriental harems. Gibbon declares[7] that the family of Proba were no exception to the rapaciousness of Count Heraclian, but were relieved of half their wealth as the price of their liberty. Augustine in a sympathetic letter to Proba, on the subject of prayer, points out the true spirit of Christian submission. He also undertook, but with poor success, to use his good offices in behalf

---

[7] Decline and Fall of the Roman Empire, Chap. XXXI.

of these and other fugitives. But the most famous sequel of the flight of this illustrious family is furnished by the announcement, two years later, that Demetrias had taken the vows of virginity. This celebrated heiress—"the foremost maiden of the Roman world for nobility and wealth," Jerome describes her—had been betrothed to a young nobleman. But, apparently acting under the counsel of Augustine, she had determined to give herself to a holy life after the manner of her age. At any rate, the conferring of the veil upon Demetrias, on the eve of her appointed wedding-day, was hailed with acclaim not only by Augustine, but by Aurelius, Jerome, Alypius, and by the renowned Pelagius, recently arrived in Carthage and soon to engage our attention. The affair made greater stir, inasmuch as a crowd of maidens, besides slaves and dependants, followed the lead of this first lady of Rome.[8]

Much more excitement and annoyance was occasioned by the presence in Hippo itself of some of these exotics of noble blood and Christian confession. There were few more remarkable Christian women in her day than the lady Melania. Abandoning her high position in Roman society she had accompanied the historian Rufinus to the East, where she finally built two monasteries. In order to escape the depredations of the barbarians, she had taken her daughter-in-law, Albina, and her granddaughter and her

---

[8] These events are set forth in Augustine's Letters, Nos. 130, 131, 150, and 188.

husband, Melania and Pinianus (whose marriage had blasted the elder Melania's hope of making a nun of her granddaughter), and settled with them in Thagaste. The entire family were inclined to the more rigid view of the religious life. They built and endowed two monasteries at Thagaste, one for thirty men, and the other for several hundred women. In other ways they lavished their wealth upon the poor, both of clergy and people. Of course they were anxious to see and converse with Augustine. But he explained to them that infirmities of body, and the jealousy of his congregation, forbade his making the journey to them. Accordingly, Pinianus and his wife visited Hippo. Their immense wealth, their piety, and their generosity, naturally won them immediate notice among the humble folk of Augustine's parish. But these same things also led soon to circumstances embarrassing, and not entirely creditable, to Augustine.

We have had occasion heretofore to make reference to the habit, in the early Church, of pressing the priestly office upon unwilling, but desirable, candidates. Pinianus seems to have anticipated some such trouble in his own case; for one of his first precautions was to exact a promise from Augustine that he should not be ordained against his wish. He was probably not surprised, therefore, when one day, during service in the Hippo Church, there arose a persistent clamor for his election and consecration to the priesthood. That would mean of course, the bestowal of his possessions upon the Church—from the worldly point of view, a most desirable end. Mindful of his promise, Augustine descended to the nave of the church, explained his situation to the people, and added that they must relinquish their demand or lose him as their bishop. This produced a temporary lull. But presently the cries were renewed, and Augustine found himself helpless. The crowd openly charged Alypius, who was present, with wishing to keep Pinianus in Thagaste. There was even danger of the church's being wrecked if the popular demand were not granted. Melania and her hapless husband had some bitter things to say about the covetous spirit of the Hipponenses, and threatened to leave Africa. This led to a side conference, after which Augustine was able to announce that the noble visitors would remain in Hippo, if the ordination was not insisted upon. This sop did not prove satisfactory. The conclusion of that day—though not of "the whole matter"—was that poor Pinianus was obliged to promise, under solemn oath, that he would not depart from that city, nor suffer ordination elsewhere.

Perhaps, in the end, we must see the more humorous side of the situation. Augustine really deserves sympathy. For, the uproar of that memorable day was sudden and violent. Either Pinianus had to take the oath, or the church had to come down, and Augustine confesses that he could not conscientiously stand by and "allow the Church which I serve to be overthrown." Only, one may justly pause to reflect with gratitude, that Christian manners have improved with the years. Still later, this unusual family fell victims to the infamous cruelty of Heraclian. Dispossessed of their wealth, their popularity in Hippo waned, and they were allowed, without a protest, to make their way to the monasteries of Palestine.

Readers of "Hypatia" are familiar with the final disillusion of Count Heraclian, and ruin of his wild ambitions. A hurried, heedless expedition to Italy met with disaster at the hands of Marinus, and revealed to its hypocritical leader his own smallness. When Marinus turned his attention to ill-governed Africa, one of his first acts was to punish Heraclian's confederates, both real and supposed. Among these Marcellinus was charged (evidently through false witnesses) with being one. He had been a vigorous opponent of the Donatists, who now, by a temporary turn of fortune, won the ear of Marinus, and brought Marcellinus to judgment. Augustine and other bishops who interceded for him, were given to understand that no further action would be taken until some bishop should hear before Honorius the case of the distinguished prisoner. But the execution took place suddenly and under the most suspicious circumstances. The fact that Augustine thereupon left Carthage "immediately and secretly" has led one author to whine, wholly without warrant, that "his behavior on the occasion is not so clear as one could wish." Surely nothing could be more "clear," or satisfactory, than Augustine's own explanation—that he could not both seek from Marinus leniency towards certain fugitive rebels who crowded the churches of Carthage, and also "rebuke him with the severity which his crime deserved." The death of Marcellinus was a personal blow to Augustine, who pays him a glowing tribute, dwelling upon his innocence, constancy, zeal, sincerity, humility, and integrity. When the emperor heard of this judicial crime, he took away from Marinus his office and banished him.

It was in this period of confusion, of shifting uncertainties, of dissolution and terror and wonder, that Augustine wrote "The City of God." Sometimes complaint is made that the soberminded bishop had lost all sympathy with the city of men, and that the wreck of Rome, therefore, did not concern him except as he might draw from it moral and spiritual lessons. One might well ask, "What better occupation could there be for a zealous bishop than spiritual use of such a calamity?" But the complaint in reality is groundless. Doubtless he was not as visibly moved as Jerome, who cried out: "A terrible rumor reaches me from the West, telling of Rome bought, besieged, life and property perishing together. My voice falters, for she is captive; that city which enthralled the world." It is certain, however, that the shock of Rome's fall did disturb Augustine. In his sermons he reverted to it often, insomuch that his people cried out, "O that he would hold his tongue about Rome!"[9] Furthermore, in the new defense of Christianity which was occasioned by the breaking up of the empire, Augustine was, as we have seen, foremost. In this he was joined by others, like Jerome, Orosius, Ambrose, and Salvian. Then, at the instigation of friends, he set himself to a wider elaboration of what he already had attempted in sermons and letters. His purpose at first was to show that it was not Rome's discarding of her old gods which had ruined her. On the contrary, the Christian religion, if duly followed, would produce the best not only of soldiers but of husbands, sons, officials, creditors. In short, the decay of Rome, as acknowledged by Sallust and other writers of earlier times, had set in long before the Christian era.[10] But, following out these ideas, Augustine's work at last expanded into a comprehensive theory of history, and became, as Ozanam has said, "the first real effort to produce a philosophy of history." With this task he was busy nearly down to the year of his death; for the composition of "The City of God" ran over thirteen or fourteen years.

This is hardly the place for a thorough-going analysis of "The City of God."[11] It is rather the

---

[9] Sermon 105: Ch. 12.　　[10] City of God, II, 18; and III, 10.

[11] If any one cares for an elaborate analysis of the book—though only the reading of the book itself can give satisfaction—it can be found in a number of places, such as, Cutts's Saint Augustine, Chap. XX, in The Fathers for English Readers; or in American Presbyterian Theological Review, Vol. III, Article by E. H. Gilbert, D. D.

circumstances of its writing which clothe it with a deathless grandeur. As Augustine pondered upon the vanished glory of the earthly city, there seemed to hover over the ruins the splendid vision of the City of God, "coming down out of heaven, adorned as a bride for her husband." Human history and human destiny were not therefore wholly identified with the history of any earthly power. Men must take profounder views of history, and see that, from the first, the community of God's people has lived side by side with the kingdom of this world. In all, there are twenty-two books. Of these, five books are given to an attack upon paganism—to use Augustine's own words, "to refute those who fancy that the polytheistic worship is necessary in order to secure worldly prosperity, and that all these overwhelming calamities have befallen us in consequence of its prohibition." The following five books are more philosophic in nature, the moral impotence of the systems of Varro and Plato coming in for unsparing criticism. In the remaining twelve books, which form the second half of the work, Augustine is led into a full treatment of his own convictions concerning such historical doctrines as the creation, the fall, the connection between the two Testaments, the incarnation, and the "last things." Of the effect produced by "The City of God" on its own age, one hesitates to judge. So great a scholar as Bengnot declares that the effect must have been only slight. But there can be no doubt of its popularity during the later ages, nor of the sanity of the judgment that this is Augustine's masterpiece. In spite of the prolixities, the verbose eloquence, the flimsy arguments, and what Erasmus charitably styled "the apparent obscurity," "The City of God" must take rank as a book of profound genius, wide horizons, vast learning, and, for the most part, unanswerable argument, "among the few greatest books of all time."[12]

The central idea of the book is the familiar contrast between the earthly city (*civitas terrena*), and the city of God (*Civitas Dei*). These two societies stand for principles and aims precisely opposite. The City of God is controlled by a love of God which extends to the contempt of self, and aspires to "heavenly peace." In the city of men, the rule is, to love self, even to the disregard of God, and to seek an earthly peace, even by the path of falsehood and force.

But who comprise this City of God? The exigencies of his contemporaneous struggle with the Pelagians determined Augustine's answer. The contrast was more than one of principles and of purposes. It was a contrast between elect and non-elect. But Augustine was at least keen enough to perceive that there could be no final and visible separation of the two in this world. Not only do the two cities depend upon one another, so that the City of God (according to Augustine) is wanting

---

[12] Marcus Dods, in Translator's Preface of City of God, Post-Nicene Fathers, Vol. II, p. 13.

in resources to give it visible power without the help of the earthly city, and the City of Men can not attain its purposes without the aid of such moral influences as are found only in the heavenly city. In addition, the Church is only a portion of the City of God; for outside the fold of the one, Augustine is willing to admit there are individuals belonging to the other. But, beyond the limits of the City of God, men cease to be good or to do good, their "virtues" being nothing more than "splendid vices."

Nevertheless, it was the ecclesiastical organization, the Church, which to Augustine stood in the world visibly, as the City of God.[13] With him, for the first time in history, the machinery of the State was called in to give potency to this organization, to make the Church irresistible. The idea of world-empire, which for hundreds of years had hung about the name of Rome, must be centralized in a new power, in order to meet the universal demand of a capricious age for absolute authority. Hitherto, the religious movement and the political movement had existed side by side. But the fall of the earthly commonwealth made way for its spiritual correlative, "the city which hath foundations, whose builder and maker is God." Thus, in its impressive organization, in its institutions, and above all, in its great councils, the City of God presented to men the aspect of a world-wide Holy Empire.

---

[13] City of God, XIX, 21.

It must not be overlooked that there is a deeper view of Augustine's idea of the kingdom of God, a view with which this one is seemingly quite inconsistent. But there can be no doubt that with him the mediæval conception of an established hierarchical system had its theoretical roots. As Mr. James Bryce has declared, in his invaluable work: "It is hardly too much to say that the Holy Roman Empire was built upon the foundation of the 'City of God.'"[14] Augustine could not have foreseen the inevitable outcome of the process to which he thus gave sanction. He hardly understood that if the empire "took its place within the Church, and the Church through it governed the world," the only result was a papacy—a new Rome, and an imperial throne of the Church. But it is easy, from our vantage-point, to see how all this came about. All that was required was to change in slight degree Augustine's ideal of the City of God—"to substitute for the reign of Christ in the soul, the familiar thought of the kingdom in the sense of an organized government," and you have "the ecclesiastical superstructure, raised by Gregory VII and Innocent III, of an omnipotent hierarchy set over nations and kingdoms, to pluck up and break down

---

[14] Bryce, The Holy Roman Empire, p. 94, f. n. 1. In the same place is found an interesting reference to the influence of the City of God upon Charles the Great: "He was delighted with all the books of St. Augustine, especially in those entitled the City of God." "One can imagine the impression which such a chapter as that on the true happiness of a Christian emperor (v. 24) would make on a pious and susceptible mind."

and to destroy, and to overthrow and to build and to plant."[15]

Professor Allen, who, in most respects, does not spare Augustine, gives his conception of the Church credit for doing two things. It proved an insuperable barrier to the wave of Mohammedanism, and it made possible the transition from the Roman Empire of his day to the papal empire of the Middle Ages.[16] This is important. Historians agree that there was no thought of antagonism to the empire in the barbarian mind. So wide-spread was the conception of empire, that the barbarians could not think in other terms. One can hardly regard it otherwise than providential, therefore, that Augustine's commanding message of a Church, universal and enduring and magnificent as the empire itself, should gain the ear of these young Germano-Roman tribes, just at that opportune time, when the rending of the old order made the existence of a new one, of equal grandeur, a necessity. The Church may deprecate the unwarrantable abuses and the

---

[15] Archibald Robertson, Regnum Dei, the Bampton Lectures, 1901. Dr. R's entire discussion of Augustine (Lecture V) seems to me searching, scholarly, and impartial.

[16] Continuity of Christian Thought, p. 169. The words are memorable: "The history of nearly a thousand years is summed up in his experience; but it was, on the whole, a history which the world does not care to see repeated, valuable as may be the results which it has contributed to secure to Christian civilization. It may have been necessary that the world should go back again to the 'beggarly elements'—but if so, it was because new races had come forward to carry on the line of human progress—who must pass under the yoke of the law before they were ready for the spirit of life and liberty. The work of Augustine ministered to this end." Cf. also Harnack, History of Dogma, V, p. 240.

shame, which have followed in the train of ideas to which Augustine gave the impulse. She may not succeed in finding full vindication for either his theories or his practices. But we must in an impartial judgment, conclude that the triumphant rise of the City of God, out of the prostrate City of Men, was due to the ardor and stern loyalty of Augustine.

CHAPTER XIII.

LABORS, LITERARY AND THEOLOGICAL.

WHATEVER may be our judgment as to the value of Augustine's thousand-and-one works,[1] we can not suppress our admiration for the mind which produced them. When one considers the variety of his subjects and the countless distractions, the wonder is, that he wrote so much of permanent worth. Most of the philosophy, the science, the theology, the knowledge of the arts, the ethics, of his day, are reflected in his writings. It is difficult to agree with one famous Frenchman in his effusive praise of Augustine, which leads him to declare that he wrote equally well on music and on free-will. The truth is, Augustine was unequal. One would not think of comparing "On the Divination of Demons" with his four books "On Christian Doctrine." But sustained grandeur is not sought in any man, of however great genius, when that man has been crowded with incessant labors through forty years. And the labors were about as varied as any man was ever called upon to assume.

---

[1] The earliest biographer of Augustine enumerates considerably over a thousand works, though he includes letters and sermons.

Preaching, traveling, acting in the capacity of judge and arbiter, answering at great length and with painstaking care the inquiries of anxious philosophers and puzzled statesmen, and pious women, by sheer ability thrusting himself to the forefront of every controversy of his age, catechising, teaching, descending to the needs of the many poor and afflicted of his congregation—thus did this man spend himself, though bearing about an extremely frail body to the end. If Carlyle's dictum were true—"I have no notion of a truly great man that could not be all sorts of men"—then Augustine would have, by that test, a just claim to greatness.

Of all that Augustine ever wrote, the living interest will continue, in the future as in the past, to center about the works that have to do with himself. There are three volumes which are of this abiding personal nature. Little more need be said of the "Letters." To them one must look for a true picture of Augustine in his manifold relations to the people and activities of his time. In them one finds the busy bishop at his work, the steadfast friend, the tender brother, the zealous Churchman, the adroit statesman, the father of the oppressed, the foe of heresy, the oracle of men and women with questions, the central figure in the Church of the fourth century. Some of the letters swelled to the proportions of serious theological treatises. Their purely literary quality perhaps ought not to be a subject of inquiry; for the letters apparently came warm from their author's heart, without any attempt at rhetorical effect. They are the utterance of a man of intense convictions, and often surprise by their narrow intolerance. But they never do violence to the grace of gentleness, unless it is when he lets loose his "lash of lightnings" to scourge some moral monstrosity of his day. Genuine literary flavor, however, is not wanting to the letters. An impressive earnestness one never fails to find. Flashes of humor, sympathy almost superhuman, epigram, simile, do a great deal to offset the tiresome prolixities and involved rhetoric. But these letters must always possess more than an obsolete interest, because they open the door for us into a life that was brotherly and warmly human to men of every degree.

As of the same autobiographic value must be mentioned the "Retractations." By this word it is not to be understood that Augustine came in later life so fully to alter his positions as to require a separate work for amendment and withdrawal. His main purpose, undertaken in his seventy-third year, was to pass his entire writings under critical review, mindful of the cheapness of mere words, and eager to eliminate any that were overhasty or inconsistent. The honesty and humility of Augustine in the "Retractions" are beyond censure. One may not be able to detect the necessity for all these revisions, and in many cases it may be equally difficult to find any choice between later and earlier statements. But the passion for truth, the unadulterated conscientiousness (never seen to purer advantage than in an old man making frank acknowledgment that he has been in the wrong), and courage, that led to the patient correction of his mistaken judgments and unfortunate phrases, win our unstinted esteem.

But as all the world knows, it is in the "Confessions" that Augustine is found at his best; for there, in praise to God for His mercy, he unreservedly pictures himself at his worst. Of that enough perhaps has been said. Soul-revelations, of the type of Rousseau's "Confessions" or Goethe's "Truth and Fiction," are of doubtful value. The question of public confession of particular guilt has been finally settled in such books as "The Scarlet Letter." Wherever one's own life is masked in hypocrisies by silence, or another life is blighted, an open confession is imperative. On the other hand, what Charles Spurgeon called positive "pollution" may result from such regrettable self-disclosures as those of the brilliant German and the forlorn Frenchman. Their lack of any worthy motive, their insincerity and affectation are not met in the "Confessions." Augustine does not pose. Nor does he dangle his sins before our eyes with the air of the soured cynic or the conscienceless dilettante. He is in manly earnest in his detestation of the voluptuousness which marred his young manhood. He has no concessions to make to that weak philosophy which looks upon such vices as a sort of stepping-stone to manhood. Rather would he join with a modern prophet in terming such a preparation for life's activities only "a kind of mud-bath," declaring that "we become men, not after we have been dissipated, and disappointed in the chase of false pleasure," not by the training we "receive in this devil's service, but only by our determining to desert from it."[2] To the last Augustine was conscious that the entanglements of his school-days formed a dark blot upon the total canvas of his life. In old age, with the gift of a copy of the "Confessions" to the distinguished Darius, he writes: "In these behold me, that you may not praise me beyond what I am."

In their passionately devotional spirit, the "Confessions" hold a place with the best work of à Kempis, Bunyan, Jeremy Taylor, and Henry Drummond. One often feels about Augustine as has been said of Samuel Rutherford, that "he was so much a lover of his Lord that, when you read his words, you think yourself eavesdropping, as if you were hearing two lovers in their gentle, wooing speech; so love-impassioned was his intimacy with Christ." Nothing could be more Christian than the spirit, which prostrates itself in shame and confusion in memory of its sin, but immediately rises in affectionate faith and assured communion with God. As Harnack describes the piety of Augustine:

---

[2] Thomas Carlyle, in the Essay on Burns.

"He preached the sincere humility which blossoms only on ruins—the ruins of self-righteousness."[3] And this humility was founded upon an oversweeping sense of his reconciliation to God through the blood of Christ alone. But that very thing determined the nature of his faith—a deep, unquestioning, happy confidence in God. It led him to call God both Father and Mother, "Thou Fairness, ancient, yet so new," "Sweetness happy and assured," or in the untranslatable words of the "Meditations:" "Dulcissime, Amantissime, Desideratissime, Pulcherrime, Tu melle dulcior, lacte et nive candidior, nectare suavior, gemmis et auro preciosior, cunctisque terrarum divitiis et honoribus mihi carior, quando Te videbo? quando satiabor de pulchritudine tua?" One never feels that such expressions, from the lips of Augustine, even approach anything like a weak sentimentality. They are the strong outpourings of a nature deeply religious. The "Confessions" do not represent manhood shorn of its vigors. They are a saint's protest that manhood, virile, pure, and in perfect balance, is possible only through union with God. Augustine has been named the father of mysticism. But his mysticism, while not lacking in ecstasy, and emotional self-repression, is always intelligent, and passes readily into the most abstract reasoning. Faith leads him to God, but also to everything else in the universe. It is the starting-point of all intel-

---

[3] History of Dogma, V, p. 65.

lectual, as well as soul, attainment. The new world into which faith ushers the soul, broadens into realms beyond the comprehension of the unbeliever. Hence, one must not be surprised to be conducted suddenly, from the warm realities of a verifiable Christian experience, in the first nine books of the "Confessions," to the chilled atmosphere of the closing books (X-XIII), in which are elaborated, in analytical and metaphysical vein, the truths of creation, the essence of God, time and eternity, and the human mind.

To these writings, of a more personal nature, must be added the polemical works of Augustine. Of this work in general, it may be said that it is remarkable for its absence of bitterness, combined with its obstinate insistence upon the correctness of its own positions. To the Manichæans he writes with the utmost tolerance: "Let neither of us assert that he has found truth; let us seek it as if it were unknown to both. For truth can be sought with zeal and unanimity, if by no rash presumption it is believed to have been already found." But presently he does not hesitate to pronounce their doctrine nonsense and absurdity.[4] Of his relation to the Donatist and Manichæan disputes I have spoken. To him belongs the credit of raising an effective barrier against the progress of the error of Mani in the West. It was his vigorous assaults, also, that

---

[4] Cf. Against the Ep. of Manichæus Called Fundamental, I, 3, and On the Profit of Believing.

finally took the heart out of the Donatist party.[5] Against the Priscillianists (a Spanish offshoot of Manichæism), he wrote two important books, and a few letters. In truth, there was no heresy of his day which Augustine did not oppose. An account of the heresies, in all eighty-eight, from Simonians to Pelagians, he set forth in a work addressed to his friend Quodvultdeus in the year 430.

Nearly all Augustine's constructive theology grew out of the exigencies of controversy. This is true of the works dealing with the Holy Spirit, the Deity of our Lord, and the Trinity. The Arian heresy had not died with the triumph of the Athanasians. To that branch of faith the Vandals and Goths had been converted. In 428, a band of these Arian Goths were sent to Africa, and one of their bishops, Maximinus, visited Hippo. Naturally, a debate took place between him and Augustine. The latter was somewhat stiff and uncompromising, which led the suave Maximinus to charge him with collusion with imperial forces. The debate was not finished, as the Arian was summoned to Carthage, where it was soon rumored that Augustine had been worsted. This resulted in a decisive work, "Against Maximinus." In the same year came forth one of Augustine's most monumental works, upon which he busied himself with studious care from the year 400 until 428. I refer to the fifteen books against the Arians, "On the Holy Trinity."

---

[5] For complete lists of the Anti-Manichæan and Anti-Donatist writings the reader is directed to Vol. IV of the Post-Nicene Fathers, edited by Prof. Philip Schaff.

To Augustine, the doctrine of the Trinity was one of those mysteries, "which, unless it were too vast for our full intellectual comprehension, would surely be too narrow for our spiritual needs."[6] In constructing the doctrine, therefore, he was more concerned to find expression for facts of experience than merely to formulate a philosophical tradition. I think it can easily be demonstrated that his work was not primarily speculative, but arose out of a desire to combine in a coherent system the full teaching of the Bible. But it is undoubtedly true that he was influenced by at least two other considerations. First, he had met with the beginnings of a doctrine of Trinity in Neo-Platonism, and had no difficulty in developing what he had learned there. This, however, can hardly be regarded as important. But the second influence was important. Probably few would care to go so far as Professor Harnack, in declaring that Augustine was obliged by tradition to formulate a theory of Trinity, and by experience to believe in one God, and that, if he had been able to make a fresh start, he never would have given the Trinity a thought.[7] But it is safe to say the traditional doctrine filled his horizon enough to determine his unyielding insistence upon its truth. Athanasius had cleared the air for those who came under the bracing influences of his thought. But that was mostly in the East.

---

[6] On the Trinity, V, 2.
[7] See the History of Dogma, Vol. IV, pp. 129-136.

Western Christianity was less given to speculation on the nature of God. Augustine himself was unfamiliar with the Greek writings on the subject, while he quotes no Latin father, except Hilary of Poictiers.

There were four problems which confronted Augustine in his development of the Trinitarian view. First, he must show that *the Triune God is one God.* In his quarter of Christendom, indeed, that was the starting-point. "We are not to speak of three gods, but one God. The Trinity is one God."[8] In an effort to preserve monotheism, the teachers of the West dwelt rather more upon the divine unity than upon the distinctions of persons in the Godhead. But, in the second place, it was also necessary to explain *how there could exist three distinct persons, with separate functions, in one undivided substance*—how there could be one God in Trinity. The Christian reply is, that the Trinitarian idea of God is a necessary idea. The God of Revelation can not be other than Triune. Augustine arrives at this conclusion by thinking of God as "Love." "When you have seen Love," he says, "you have seen the Trinity." To such modern questions as those of personality, he did not give a profound or definite answer. "It is necessary that these three should have a specific name, which yet is not to be found" (a view which, with Anselm, becomes, "Three, I know not what").[9]

---

[8] On the Trinity, V, 9, 12.   [9] Ibid. VII, 7.

A third question then arose: *To what extent can one believe in subordination,* and still hold fast to Trinity? In effect, Augustine ruled out the Christian idea of subordination. The Father, though "the Fountainhead of Deity," stood higher than the Son only in being unbegotten, and the Son was inferior only in having taken on a human nature through the Incarnation.[10] Similarly, the Holy Spirit, proceeding from both Father and Son, holds an inferior place to both. Of that "personal peculiarity of each person in the Trinity"—the "origination" of the Father, the "self-assertive obedience" of the Son, the "personal self-effacement" of the Holy Spirit—of which a present-day teacher so finely bears witness,[11] Augustine has nothing to say. Subordination with him is rather formal and legal, than essential.

Augustine's fourth problem was to explain how there could be such a thing as *the generation of an eternal Son.* The clear solution given by Athanasius seemingly was unknown to the bishop of Hippo. Waving all physical analogies, such as would imply a division of the Divine substance, Athanasius dwells upon the necessity of the Son of God being Son by nature. His begetting is an

---

[10] This can be verified in a number of places: e. g., XV, 31; II, 2.

[11] Professor Olin A. Curtis, in The Christian Faith, p. 502. Dr. Curtis's entire discussion of The Christian Doctrine of the Trinity (chapter XXXVI) is the most spiritual and robust of which the author knows.

inward process, the outcome of which lies in the eternal nature of God—God's Fatherhood is eternally of His own essential Being. Augustine's attempt to set forth all this, by the use of such images as light and its radiance, or fountain and stream, results only in confusion.

In forming his doctrine, Augustine had recourse to both Scripture and reason. It must be admitted, however, that his effort, to put a philosophy underneath his doctrine of Trinity, is a trifle more satisfactory. In the constitution of the soul he thought he found some image of the Trinity. As self-consciousness can arise only when an image of the memory is stamped, by the will, upon the mind, Augustine saw in these relations, of memory, will, and intellect, the Father, the Son, and the Holy Spirit. But, as Professor Ottley points out, this is to emphasize the relationships of the three persons rather than their personal distinctions.[12] Only, it must be said in fairness to Augustine, that he constantly calls attention to the imperfection and inadequacy of these ingenious analogies. Professor Harnack calls the discussions of this sort "extraordinarily acute"—a statement which might have been moderated in the interests of truth. They are clever, but hardly profound. They did supply "subsequent centuries with a philosophical education," but subsequent centuries might have been better off without them.

---

[12] R. L. Ottley, M. A., in The Doctrine of the Incarnation, Vol. II, pp. 249 ff.

In short, Augustine's Trinity is undeniably modalistic. He gives us "a Trinity of powers and functions in the one Person, and not a Trinity of personal distinctions."[13] He himself disclaimed being a "modalist." But it can not be said that he succeeded, from a philosophical point of view, in getting far beyond an idea of God as One, "with three successive and exclusive historic attitudes." His influence upon the later understanding of the doctrine is unquestionable. In the creed called "Athanasian," there is a clear trace of his characteristic methods of thought. His book became a treasure-store of the Middle Ages, and "contains Scholasticism." But that is hardly to its credit. Probably the Trinitarian situation to-day would be vastly improved could it be cleared of modes of thought that go back directly to Augustine.

It might be supposed that Augustine would produce some sort of theological system, so as to include all his ideas of Christianity in a total view. The nearest he ever came to this was in the "Enchiridion," or "Hand-Book," addressed to Laurentius. The book was primarily, however, only a review of Catholic doctrine. No attempt need be made at analysis of the "Enchiridion," as the table of contents is accessible to the English reader, and so full as readily to yield the nature of the book. In most respects the "Enchiridion" would be called

---

[13] Professor James Orr, The Christian View of God and the World, p. 271.

orthodox—merely an adequate, compact expression of what Christians believe. But there are some peculiarities of teaching that require examination.

What has Augustine to say about Christ? Practically he rested upon Him alone for the hope of salvation. But, in seeking a basis for his faith, he fails to lay hold of the difficulties of the Incarnation. His interest in such problems seems more religious than deeply intellectual. He is content with the traditions of the Church. When he is excited by the marvel of Christ's life, he falls back easily upon God's infinite power. If he must ask how the man Christ Jesus can bear about the dignity of the Son of God, it is clearly a remarkable display of the Divine grace. Seemingly it does not occur to him to begin in the Pauline way. Had he thoroughly and finally settled the question of the nature of the Son of God, many of the questions of the Humiliation would already have been answered.

The same, almost, may be said of Augustine's views of Redemption. Of "theories" he knew little. A close connection he acknowledges between Christ's death and the forgiveness of sins. The efficacy of this death consists in its fitness as a ransom to the devil, who, by the fall, secured a sort of legal right to human souls. In this Marcionite doctrine of price and barter, Augustine does not go to the disgusting lengths of later theology.[14] But he

---

[14] Gregory I, e. g., calls Christ's humanity the bait: the devil (fish) snapped at it, and was left dangling on the unseen hook, Christ's divinity.

resorts to the same figures with approval. His favorite theme in Redemption, however, is the humiliation, and example of Christ, which have power to subdue our broken natures. "When sin had placed a wide gulf between God and the human race, it was expedient that a Mediator, who, alone of the human race, was born, lived, and died without sin, should reconcile us to God, in order that the pride of man might be exposed and cured through the humility of God; that man might be shown how far he had departed from God, when God became incarnate to bring him back; that an example might be set to disobedient man in the life of obedience of the God-man."[15] This of course does not touch the borders of the deep, moral questions involved in the Atonement. At best, it is but a devotional presentation of the "moral-influence" view of Christ's sacrifice.

Another peculiarity of the "Enchiridion" is the view of remission of sins. Forgiveness is built upon penance (which, in turn, is provided for by the penitential seasons instituted by the Church), and is really reserved for the future judgment. Thus personal assurance is curtailed. With penance, almsgiving co-operates to save the sinner, though all good works issue from an inner transformation. True, there is an insistence that men are saved only "on account of their faith in Christ." But who can not easily detect the germs of Roman-

---

[15] Enchiridion, 108.

Augustine: The Thinker.

Perhaps they appear even more clearly in
ching about purgatory—though the purging
 this intermediate state are limited to those
 life have believed. Most of all, as showing
ɔmanizing tendency in Augustine, he leaned
lly to a belief in "the benefit to the souls of
ɪd from the sacraments and alms of their
friends."

: closer student of Augustine must also be-
amiliar with a mass of similar works of this
:ic and philosophical nature. Among these
: following: "On the Care of the Dead,"
. about 420; "On the Catechetical Instruction
Ignorant," 400; "On Faith and the Creed,"
ɔn the Christian Combat," 396; "On Various
ɔns of Simplicianus," 397; "On Faith in the
ɪ," 400; "On Faith and Works," 413; "On
:e," 418; special sermons, such as "On the
' "On the Fourth Day," "On the Flood," "On
rbarian Epoch," "On the Use of Fasting,"
ɔn the Destruction of the City."

:n, there is Augustine's work as a commenta-
ɪ the main, he followed his own fixed princi-
 exegesis, as set forth in the book "On Chris-
ɔoctrine." The "rule of faith" was the
ɪent of all right interpretation. If pas-
were obscure, they must be explained by
luminous ones; if a literal meaning were
ve, one must use the allegorical method.
' which comes to light in the two vol-

umes of "Commentaries." A literal explanation of Genesis, for example, was attempted in his earlier years, but abandoned for a more "spiritual," but unedifying, interpretation which was not finished till the year 415. There were also two commentaries on the Heptateuch, and the "Annotations" to Job, of Old Testament works. In the New Testament, Augustine devoted himself to the Sermon on the Mount, Romans, and Galatians, a "Harmony of the Gospels," and the Fourth Gospel. Toward the close of his life he wrote an outline of the teaching of the entire Bible, and called it "The Mirror of Holy Scripture." But his most enduring work of this kind was the "Commentary on the Psalms," most of which was given in the form of sermons. It will endure, that is, mostly because of its lively appreciation of spiritual realities, not for any marked exegetical values.

Finally, there is still a peculiar interest in the various moral and ascetic treatises of Augustine. His own practice, leaving aside the question of his relation to the mother of his son, involved him in self-denial and life-engulfing consecration. But his theories, of voluntary celibacy and poverty, the world has already condemned. We can not follow him, except in the spirit which impelled him to write the works "On Virginity," "On Conjugal Love," "On Continence," "On Marriage," "On the Blessedness of Widowhood," and "On Lying," though the two last reflect an ethical passion which excites the admiration. Augustine never caught a glimpse of the glory of the Christian family. He lived in an age of awful sexual excesses, and his soul, like that of the fathers in general, revolted, finding rest in an undivided service of Christ and His Church.

In this survey (perhaps too extended, but, even so, inadequate) we have been able to judge Augustine's qualities in a great variety of situations. He was human, and lived under the pressure of many unavoidable and unfortunate conditions. Hence, we must pass a charitable judgment upon his defects, while we lament the evils that grew from them, and hold up for praise the truly noble attainments which offset them.

CHAPTER XIV.

THE PELAGIANS.

During the twenty years, from 410 down to the very day of his death, there were three men who occasioned Augustine a great deal of trouble. One was the monk known in history by the name Pelagius. In all probability he was a Briton. Jerome, always more picturesque than exact, calls him "the great, fat Albion dog." He was alluding to the well-known corporeal dimensions of Pelagius, whom he describes in another place by the vulgar phrase, "protruding with the porridge of the Picts." At any rate, if the British monk might justly be charged with being a good eater, he seems to have practiced a commendable self-restraint in other respects. When we find him first in Rome, early in the fifth century (being unattached to any monastery), he was a man of devout and virtuous character, a professor of Christianity, and noted for his zeal in winning converts to the faith. Preaching as he did a rigid asceticism, he naturally found himself in antagonism to the corruption and laxity of the Roman Church. When he chided, he was met with the excuse that human nature is weak. Such excuses became intolerable to him. "O blind madness," was his outcry, "we accuse God of forgetting the human weakness of which He Himself is the author, and imposing laws on man which he can not endure." The blameless life, he declared, was the possible life because it was the necessary life. It was his custom in preaching, therefore, to begin by showing the inherent power of man's nature. It was in this way he came in conflict with the teaching of Augustine. He heard it said one day that the great bishop had written, in the "Confessions," this prayer: "Give what thou commandest, and command what Thou wilt." Pelagius met this saying with a passionate denial of its truth. "I say that man is able to be without sin, and that he is able to keep the commandments of God." This seems to have been with him an honest conviction. Apparently he had been called upon to fight no battles for purity. He was possessed of a mind quite in sympathy with truth, and had been able to discipline his nature into harmony with moral order.[1]

Pelagius had one great success in Rome. He won over to his views the Roman lawyer Cœlestius. This man, unlike his teacher, had the fire of youth, and besides brought to the new doctrine a considerable argumentative ability. He and Pelagius fled from Rome some time during the general unrest of 409 and 410. In the following year they landed in Africa and proceeded to Hippo. Just at that

---

[1] Cf. Principal Rainy, The Ancient Catholic Church, p 470.

time, the Donatist controversy was at its height, and Augustine was absent in Carthage controlling the course of the great conference. Owing to this preoccupation, therefore, there was no open meeting between the future protagonists, though they saw one another. Shortly thereafter, Pelagius set out for Palestine. It was the impulsive Cœlestius, therefore, who was first to sound in Africa the new notes of morality, free-will, and reason. The third Pelagian of note was Julian, the young Bishop of Eclanum. He, however, did not identify himself with the heresy till 418, but brought with him a philosophic mind, a readiness of expression, and a vigor in debate that taxed all the resources of Augustine. The teachings of these men burst with sudden and startling energy upon the Church of Augustine's day. Settlement had been made in the two previous centuries of the doctrines of God. But the doctrine of man and sin was still in a formative state. The newness of the assertions of Pelagius consisted not so much in his stress upon free will, as upon his denial of the demoralization of the race, and the need of Divine help. It is true that in the Western Church there had been a deeper sense of the tragic misery and ruin of sin, while in the East a kind of guard had been placed upon the lips lest one should speak openly of a corrupt human nature. But the extreme utterances of Pelagius were beyond doubt a novelty.

To get the substance of the dispute before us at

once, what claims did the Pelagians set forth? Let Augustine himself give us a brief answer.[2]

Fundamental with them was their proclamation of the dignity and perfection of human nature in every man at his birth. Thus, they arrayed themselves against any idea of original sin. Then they went a step farther, and declared for the unsullied purity of marriage and the sexual relation, as against the idea of a transmission of hereditary taint. In the third place, there was with the Pelagians an insistence upon the possibility, at all times, of a free exercise of the human will, so that the co-operation of Divine grace was rendered unnecessary. Finally, the notion of universal sinfulness, was offset by that of the sanctification of saints. In these tenets, other points, of course, were involved, as will appear. I think it can hardly be shown that Wesley was wholly correct in his summary judgment that "the real heresy of Pelagius was neither more nor less than this: the holding that Christians may, *by the grace of God* (not without it; that I take to be a mere slander) 'fulfill the law of Christ.'" The Pelagians did make profession of belief in "Grace," but they meant something very different from the evangelical grace of which Augustine makes so much.[3]

Of the outward course of the controversy, and of Augustine's part in it, only the most important

---
[2] From the work of Augustine, Against Two Letters of the Pelagians.
[3] Cf. with this Hurst, Vol. I, p. 459, footnote.

events can be mentioned. But it must be borne in mind that he was active almost without intermission, preaching, and debating, and directing a large correspondence, besides issuing the numerous and exhaustive treatises against Pelagianism.

Shortly after the departure of Pelagius for the East, Cœlestius sought ordination as a presbyter at Carthage. He was challenged by Paulinus, a deacon, and summoned before a synod under the presidency of Bishop Aurelius. Ultimately, he was excommunicated, charged with heresy on seven counts: that Adam was created mortal and would have died even if he had not sinned; that his sin entailed no guilt upon others; that infants are born in the state in which Adam was before the fall; that, even without baptism, they have eternal life; that the whole race does not die in Adam nor rise in Christ; that through the law as well as the Gospel, is entrance into the kingdom of heaven; and that there were before Christ men living without sin. Justice requires us to recognize the ethical considerations which lay beneath these contentions of Cœlestius. It was not merely the Pelagian idea of human power and freedom which stirred him. He felt the injustice of punishing a whole race for one man's faults, and the awful cruelty of damning helpless infants for want of a rite, and the peril of denying the freedom of the will, lest human responsibility be crushed out with the denial. To Augustine, who was ready to beat down anything which stood like a human pretension mocking the sovereign grace of God, these moral concerns apparently counted for nothing. Between them on the one hand, and the corruption of the heart of man and the majesty of the irresistible will of God on the other, he could see no reconciliation. And the Divine purpose must stand at all cost.

Cœlestius fled East, but not until he had made converts. Augustine had not shared in the deliberations of the synod of Carthage. But it was impossible for him to turn a deaf ear to the presence, in Africa, of the Pelagian heresy in full blast. As if expecting it after a life-long preparation, he leaped into the controversy at once. By sermon and letter he tried to interpose a quiet, persistent barrier to the theories rapidly increasing in popularity. One commendable feature of this first work of 412, was the patience and equipoise with which Augustine proceeded. His policy was not to mention the names of Pelagius and the fiery Cœlestius, but rather to bring to judgment their teachings.

In that same year, Marcellinus, who will be remembered as the presiding officer of the Donatist conference, during the previous year, sent to Augustine a number of questions bearing upon the Pelagian doctrine. He wished to know Augustine's opinion concerning the relation of death and sin, the transmission of sin, and the possibility of a life without sin. But his special eagerness was for light on the subject of infant baptism, for this had become one of the crucial tests of the debate. Augustine replied in three books On the Merits and Remission of Sins, and on the Baptism of Infants. His answer to the chief question of Marcellinus is coupled with a long dissertation on original sin as deduced from the universal reign of death. As to a life of sinless perfection, he says there is the possibility of one, but such was never lived. Then he lays down his famous dicta about infants. "The universal practice of baptizing them is an acknowledgment of their sin. Moreover, if unbaptized, they can not be with Christ; and 'He that is not with Me is against Me.' Therefore, though there is a lighter punishment for infants, they must, in case of death, be forever with the devil." Marcellinus complained that there were weighty moral objections to such an argument. But Augustine stood his ground as being based on Revelation, which closed the reasons of men.

But Marcellinus had another perplexity. He could not understand how, if it was possible for men to live sinless lives with Divine aid, there had never been such a life except in the case of Mary. This difficulty brought forth from the watchful Augustine another important work, "On the Spirit and the Letter," written also in 412. This treatise has been praised as telling us most, next to the "Confessions," "of the thoughts of that rich, profound, and affectionate mind on the soul's relations to its God."[4] What is meant is, that Augustine surpassed himself in exalting the necessity of grace. A distinction must be made, he said, between the Scripture and the light of conscience, on one side and the need of a spirit-given assistance. The former, the letter, kills, but the spirit gives light. All the light a man has may serve simply to set out, in more glaring prominence, his divergence from his moral standard and his need of higher help.

But, already, the heat of the controversy was transferred from West to East. Augustine at this time, 415, was well-nigh bewildered by overwork. But he was always accessible. From the remotest borders of Spain came a youth of burning zeal, Orosius, to get some of his questions answered; for, when he had sought elsewhere, he had been told, "Augustine is the man." He found the bishop sympathetic, but not anxious to attack any new opinions, and was content to receive from Augustine a letter to Jerome. Accordingly, he put forth on his further quest. Augustine also sent word to Jerome on a question of his own, about the origin of souls, entreating the old monk for a reply. But Jerome was in one of his moods, and replied that he had no leisure for such problems. This, however, was not the end of the mission of Orosius. Once in Jerusalem, he became the accuser of Pelagius before the synod of clergy under Bishop John.

---

[4] Canon Bright, in Introduction to Select Anti-Pelagian Treatises, XX.

Pelagius also was present. The young Spaniard recited the facts relating to the excommunication of Cœlestius and described Augustine's writings against the new theories. This was met, on the part of Pelagius, by a sullen denial of any obligations to Augustine. Bishop John was compelled to quiet the disputants at this point, and bade them go on in peace. At length, Pelagius was acquitted, and Orosius retired to the shelter of the angered Jerome. News of the affair was soon at the ears of Augustine through an epistle of Pelagius, in which he arrogantly declared he had "shut the mouth of opposition in confusion."

Augustine wisely awaited the return of Orosius, although he must have become restless, as the poisonous report went round that Pelagius had been voted orthodox by fourteen bishops. He was loath to press the case against Pelagius, admitting as he did, the unimpeachableness of his character. But he saw distinctly that it was time for decisive action. Hurrying to Carthage, he arranged for councils both there and at Mileve. Letters from Jerome, and from two Gallic bishops, Heros and Lazarus, had been brought home by Orosius meantime, and these, with other documents, were presented to the Council of Carthage late in 416. The outcome was, that the sixty-nine bishops decided to anathematize both Pelagius and Cœlestius, and to present the whole case to the Roman bishop. A similar decision was arrived at by the sixty-one bishops at

Mileve. Three letters, the last of a more private nature, were written to Innocent, of Rome. They appear among Augustine's "Letters," and are mainly his composition. It was Pelagius's denial of grace that largely formed the charge against him. The bishops at Jerusalem apparently had misunderstood his definitions, for certainly the practical outcome of human self-sufficiency would be the abandonment of both Church and sacraments. It was suggested to Innocent that he send for Pelagius, and subject him to a searching examination.

Naturally, a pause is demanded by this appeal to the Roman bishop. Time and again it has been offered as a proof of pontifical prerogatives and supremacy. From events yet to be narrated, it will be seen that, as a matter of history, the African Church was thoroughly independent of Rome. Augustine himself has in no place any word which hints at a belief in anything like the later papal authority. As historians have shown sufficiently, this particular recommendation to Rome was an expedient. In Rome the heresy had begun, and had become widespread. For many reasons, the Roman Church was the important center of Catholicism. If Pelagianism were stamped out there, it would be a decisive result for the rest of the Church.[5] Au-

---

[5] I give here a helpful note from Prof. John A. Faulkner, taken from my notebook of 1901: Six causes of Roman supremacy: 1. Rome's firmness in maintenance of the faith; no heresies. 2. Her hospitality and generosity, wealth and benefactions. 3. The influence of Paul and Peter in Rome. 4. Rome as capital of the empire; power of an idea; the influence of secular divisions on Church polity; people resorted thither. 5. Literary helps; Clementine recognitions; forgeries; Cyprian, Unity of the Church; Irenæus. 6. The claims of Rome.

gustine also suggests, in his third letter (No. 177), that the well-known character and ability of Innocent would be of great weight in determining the issue of the controversy.

It is not surprising that Innocent received the African appeal with self-complacent exultation. His three replies are repellently boastful. McCabe says, facetiously, that Innocent "takes remarkable pains to point out that they are following the time-honored custom of appealing to Rome, whilst his delight at the novelty floods" all the letters. At all events, he rewarded Augustine's flatteries by declaring Pelagius and Cœlestius deprived of the communion of the Church, until they should "recover their senses from the wiles of the devil, by whom they are held captive." Now that both Rome and Africa had frowned on the errors of the Pelagians, Augustine had reason both for rejoicing, and for confidence of his final victory. In a celebrated and much misquoted sermon (No. 131), he expressed his jubilation, and hoped that before long this disturbance of the Church would cease.[6]

But by this time, as a sort of prelude of coming events, news reached Hippo of the full proceedings of the council at Diospolis, at which Pelagius was acquitted a second time. These records are important as showing that Pelagianism made a favorable impression upon the East, not because

---

6 His exact words were: "Already two councils have, in this cause, sent letters to the Apostolic See, whence also rescripts have come back. The cause is ended; would that the error might some day end!'

the Eastern mind was more inclined in the direction of that "worldly philosophy" (as Augustine termed it), but because Pelagius actually explained away or repudiated his heresy before his judges. They also bring to light an outrage which is charged against the sympathizers of Pelagius. Shortly after his acquittal, the cloister of Jerome at Bethlehem was laid under siege, some buildings were destroyed, and several servants were killed. Augustine sternly rebuked this perpetration.

In fact, more stressful times were already at hand. A Greek, Zosimus, had succeeded Innocent upon his death in March, 417. Cœlestius, led to believe that the Eastern mind was more receptive to his views, made an effort to have himself and Pelagius reinstated. He visited Rome in September, and made a direct appeal to the bishop. Zosimus seems to have had little or no interest in theological niceties. Failing to rally his refractory clergy, he held back his decision in the case of Cœlestius, but wrote to Africa, rebuking the Church there for its too-consuming zeal in passing so severe a judgment. In like manner Pelagius had sent a remonstrance to the "Apostolic See." His defense of himself, as Zosimus afterwards informed Augustine's party, almost produced tears among the members of the Roman synod. They were deeply grieved that so virtuous a man should be thus abused, and ended by declaring Pelagius "a good Catholic of undoubted faith."

These communications from Zosimus were not likely to create the best kind of feeling in Africa. A council met in Carthage early the following year. Augustine was in the forefront. It was stoutly and summarily decreed that the case of Pelagius and his young disciple should be regarded as closed, until they should recant. By this time Zosimus had found his bearing. He replied that the African Church must not take too literally his remarks on the case of Cœlestius. His final word had not yet been spoken. Indeed, he was considering new evidence which would probably lead him to a reversal of sentiment. This message was read before the second Council of Carthage, late in April. Over two hundred bishops were in attendance. The unlooked-for mildness of Zosimus modified their plans and they were content with passing a series of canons against Pelagianism. These they forwarded to Rome to confirm the wavering bishop's faith.

One writer regards as "a remarkable piece of engineering," on Augustine's part, certain events which occurred almost simultaneously with "the great African Council"—events which probably had considerable weight in determining Zosimus's change of heart. If there is no direct proof that Augustine was instrumental in obtaining the intervention of State aid, at this juncture, the evidence certainly points towards him. In any case, the Emperor Honorius sent forth an order, just before the Carthaginian Council met, throwing on the side of the African Church the influence of imperial authority. It was not the first time Augustine had resorted to civil penalty for heresy, and it is known he was in correspondence with powerful friends at court. The effect of the decree was to send into exile the leaders of the heresy, and to confiscate their goods.

About this time, Augustine began to busy himself with more pretentious literary refutations of the false doctrine. A notable case is his renewed relations with Pinianus and Melania. It will be remembered that these noble persons, under adverse fortune, had left Hippo (their departure being little to the credit of Augustine's Church), and settled in a monastery at Bethlehem. There, at length, they came in contact with Pelagius, and besought him to renounce his reputed errors. To their surprise, he boldly denounced "the man who says that the grace of God, whereby Christ came into the world to save sinners, is not necessary, not only every hour, but for every act of our lives." He read to them from his book, moreover, his opinion that infants should be baptized in the same manner as adults. Thus artfully did he seek to draw them into his net. They thought it best, however, to seek the counsel of Augustine, and he replied by writing two books, "On the Grace of Christ," and "On Original Sin" (418). In the former he denies Pelagius's pretense about grace, declaring that the monk has no conception of grace, except as Revelation and the example of Christ. During all this period of "sharpest conflict" with the Pelagians, it must be remembered that Augustine was preaching incessantly. His pen also was never weary of letter-writing. Among the significant series of letters in his collection are those which passed between him and the presbyter Sixtus, afterwards Pope Sixtus III.

It is with the year 420 that Julian, of Eclanum, comes into view. In condemning the Pelagians, Zosimus had threatened with expulsion from their bishoprics those of his clergy who did not subscribe to Augustinian principles. Among the first to refuse was Julian. His first attack was upon the work concerning marriage. He was vehement in his charges. He accused Augustine of returning to Manichæism in his idea of a corrupt nature, and declared that the doctrine of predestination led to fatalism. He demanded a proper rehearing of the whole case before a regular council.

Pope Boniface, who had followed Zosimus, referred Julian's defense of himself to the attention of Augustine. He, in turn, published an elaborate examination of the questions involved under the title, "Against Two Letters of the Pelagians." In this work, Augustine took up one by one the separate items in Julian's indictment. No sooner had he finished, than he was made acquainted with the full nature of his new opponent's attack, and proceeded promptly to express himself with greater force, and at greater length, than before, in a book entitled "Against Julian," which one admirer has described as "almost divine." Few of the saints have suffered more from the servile flatteries of intemperate friends than Augustine. There were numerous interruptions to a second massive work against the same incorrigible young heresiarch, so that, until the very close of his career, Augustine was engaged upon the book which bares the significant title, "The Unfinished Work." We can not honestly regret the failure to prolong this work; for in reality, there are now more of the same sort than any one (save a very limited coterie) ever reads. But Augustine's courage, which kept him at his indefatigable labors until the Vandals thundered almost at his study-door, deserves a passing tribute of respect.

These last years of the bishop's life were crowned with several of his most noteworthy anti-Pelagian treatises. About 426, he sent the "Enchiridion" out into the world, intending it not merely as a hand-book on religion, but as a calm survey of the truth denied and made void by his antagonists. Soon after he tried to quiet the strife of the monastery of Adrumentum by such expositions of doctrine as are found in his larger work, "On Grace and Free Will." The monks at Adrumentum, however, were inclined to a certain amount of free-thinking, which led them to question the admissibility of all "Lord Pope Augustine" (as they called him) had to say on the subject of sovereign grace. With no little human passion, they wished to know how it came about that, if all good was from God's grace, man could be rebuked for not doing what he could not do? A reply was made in another work, "On Rebuke and Grace," in which Augustine endeavors to make clear that the supremacy of Divine grace does not supersede human duty. "We deserve rebuke for our very unwillingness to be rebuked," is his uncompromising declaration. Of this more will be said in the next chapter. Already, the atmosphere was clearing of the extreme Pelagian views, and a middle school of "semi-Pelagians" was beginning to make itself felt. Against the representatives of this new movement, at the instigation of two laymen, Prosper and Hilary, Augustine wrote two books which go under the separate title of "On the Predestination of the Saints," and "The Gift of Perseverance." These are the best evidences we have of the strength of his mental powers in their full maturity. The heresy outlived Augustine. Traces of it linger until the close of the century. But at an Œcumenical Council of Ephesus, in 431, pure Pelagianism received the final condemnation of both East and West.[7]

It is perhaps a misfortune that the student of this controversy is obliged to rely almost wholly upon the writings of Augustine, in order to get his understanding of the peculiarities of belief on the other side. But we can, even so, approximate a truthful

---

[7] Cf. Prin. Rainy, Ancient Catholic Church, p. 473, f. n. 2.

survey of Pelagian teaching. The fundamental point was that free will remains unimpaired by the fall. This power of choice itself was acknowledged as a gift of God, but its use in practical action was man's prerogative. This implied, moreover, that no corruption had been transmitted from the first man to his offspring of the race. If the battle is harder for men now, it is not because they are not born with the same moral powers with which Adam was endowed, but because appeals to the appetites of men have increased with the centuries. And it certainly was untenable (they said) to charge the guilt of Adam to any one except himself.

Pelagius and his disciples also had a conception of grace. But it is certain they meant nothing like a work of the Holy Spirit upon the nature of man. At most it was a vague confession of benefits of God's goodness—the remission of sins, the Divine revelation (especially the example of Christ), and ability to act freely in the choice of good. There were considerations minor to these. But the root of the trouble was the assertion of an absolutely unfettered will in every man.

Augustine's doctrine of grace was formulated under the stress of controversy, but was simply an outgrowth of previous convictions. These had resulted from an examination of the Epistles of Paul, especially Romans and Corinthians. In his earlier career he had held that man is dependent on Divine help for salvation, but that faith is man's own spontaneous act. But he came to believe that it was both presumption and an impossibility for man's relations with God to originate in free-will. Thus he settled down to an irreversible conviction that men live under an absolute necessity of grace for their salvation.

This necessity arose from the helpless condition of the race through Adam's transgression. Augustine conceived that the first man's fall involves the entire race, not by any arbitrary constitution, but because the entire race, potentially, was present in its progenitor, and therefore shares with him his guilt, as well as his perdition. Men are not dispossessed of their powers of choice. They are still "free." But they are left with no desire for anything but evil, and can therefore choose nothing good. It is clear from this, so the argument goes, that any renewal of man's nature must begin in the omnipotence of God.

Grace is God's means of providing and bringing near to men the gift of His salvation. With Augustine it is the first and last word of the Gospel. He describes it sometimes as *prevenient,* meaning that it influences and enables us to make right choices. It is also *co-operative,* since it works with the good will so soon as we have one. In addition, it is *irresistible.* God holds it utterly in His power to bestow His favors where He will. He does so not regardless of all laws, but by providential use of them. Whatever the obstacle, His grace at last must overcome it, if it sets out to. Above all, grace is *gratuitous*. It comes to us totally without our choice or desert.

Upon whom, then, in the view of Augustine, is the grace of God bestowed? Our answer must keep in sight the ideas of man as "a mass of ruin," and of grace as gratuitous. It follows from the unmitigated and self-imposed ruin of mankind, that they have no claim whatever upon the mercy of God. If He should leave them to perish, it would be only justice. Consequently, there is no injustice in His choosing this one and that, as the objects of His unmerited favor. And this bestowal of grace is not uncertain, for it proceeds according to God's foreknown purpose. Predestination, in the thought of Augustine, was God's sovereign grace winning whom it would to the fold of God. Once brought into the fold, this grace carried them irresistibly through all the trials of life, and made their perseverance to the end a certainty.

Surveying the wide field from the side of ethics, it must appear that Pelagius was nearer the truth than Augustine, though both erred broadly. It can not be maintained, of course, that men are free to choose the course of right always. Nothing is truer of life than the fact of moral conflict, most present and poignant to the man of high ideals who has not learned the way to Christian victory. But where does the turning-point lie? Is it in man's free will, or in God's generous grace? It is claimed man is helpless to choose; that his ruin has left him deprived of power even to accept a proffered Divine help. But what moral meaning can there be to his failure to choose Christ, let us say, if he is not responsible for his failure? And how can responsibility be urged where there is no moral freedom? A proper Augustinian reply, probably, would be, that there *is* responsibility—for the helplessness in which his share of Adam's guilt involves him; for every man is born a ruined sinner. But such answers, unfortunately, make no account of the yawning difference between personal sin and racial sin. The modern doctrine of heredity is made much of by disciples of Augustine.[8] But there is nothing consonant with that doctrine in the theory of the transmission of guilt. It is depravity, not demerit, which is handed down from parent to child. Never can an unbiased judgment see anything right in a man's being held responsible for what is not personally and finally *his*. And Augustine's older contemporary, the eloquent Chrysostom, proclaimed a more wholesome and satisfying message, when he taught that the will of man, though impaired by the fall, has still the power to accept or reject the offer of salvation. This brings the crisis of man's turning to God where, ethically, it should be—in his own will. In this, moreover, the Scriptures undoubtedly concur. There is no denial of

---

[8] See, e. g., Prof. James Orr, The Progress of Dogma, pp. 150 ff.

grace in such a position, but a glorious exaltation of it.

But it was inevitable with Augustine, that, having taken his stand on the declaration of man's complete moral ruin, he should pass on to his idea of the Divine method of saving people out of their corruptions. Divine election is indispensable in saving men who have no moral powers of their own. But, first, is it a defensible method? And then, is it possible? It is not enough to say God's ways are inscrutable, but must be just. Nor is there any help in the more recent way of offsetting the horror of the doctrine by painting a white background of love in God. The fact remains, whether it sounds well to say so or not, that the Augustinian notion of unconditional predestination is arbitrary and indefensible. If it is said that none have any claim whatever upon God's grace, and that therefore God is not unjust in "passing by" some, the quick reply is that, on the broad level of no claim, justice requires that all should be treated alike, and not that some should be treated as if they possessed claims.

But, is unconditional election possible? Can God override the wills of men? Is grace irresistible? Is it possible for God to break down, as Professor Orr suggests, even the desire to resist the good? What moral meaning is there, then, to faith? Such questions ought to be answered in the asking.

Augustine was in sorest straits when he attempted to weld into one his theories of the Church and the doctrine of grace. Plainly it was the visible Church which was the only adequate representation of God's purpose in salvation. Here were His elect. But, were none saved outside the visible Church? At this point Augustine halted. But then he pushed his conclusions to their end: "He that has not the Church as his mother, has not God for his Father." And unbaptized infants? The step was unavoidable: "All those who die unbaptized, including infants, are finally lost and depart into eternal punishment," (though mercifully, "the place of lightest punishment in hell is assigned to those who were guilty of no sin but original sin").

The heresy of Pelagius was a dangerous one. But it was not to be met by Augustine's no doubt zealous, but nevertheless distorted views. There *is* such a thing as predestination, and it concerns the salvation of men. But it is accompanied by a universal appeal to men, and is based through foreknowledge, upon the freely-made choices of men under the pressure of the Holy Spirit. Such foreordination is truly Pauline, and answers to a deep Christian experience of the undeserved riches of God's ineffable grace, in making so magnificent a provision.

CHAPTER XV.

AUGUSTINE AND THE FINAL STRUGGLE.

Not till the year after Augustine's death did the Œcumenical Council at Ephesus, pass final adverse judgment upon the views of Pelagius. But, as we have seen, out of the ashes had already sprung a mild compromise, which was destined to run its course for many years, and to come to us under the name of semi-Pelagianism. As this was a protest against the more exaggerated ideas of Augustine, it was inevitable that he should be drawn into the contest which ensued.

A form of compromise, between the harsher features of Augustinianism and the unscriptural ground of Pelagius, was attempted by the monk Cassian, whose monastery was in Southern Gaul. Cassian was ready to admit the universal need of Divine grace for salvation. But he protested that men could resist God's grace, or could freely turn to Him, and that grace was not granted without regard to merit, while God's predestination was only fatalism. In the two works which this new heresy called forth, "On the Predestination of the Saints," and "The Gift of Perseverance," Augustine endeavored in a final effort to make clear his position. But it can not be said that he succeeded in making his favorite doctrine of predestination at all attractive. No objection, he said, could be made against predestination that did not lie with equal strength against grace. But he failed to see, as usual, that there can be no grace in giving, unless there is free will in receiving.

Of kindred interest is Augustine's relations at this time with another monk from the south of France, a certain Leporius. This man, according to report, had been condemned in his native country, because of his leanings toward Pelagianism. Accordingly he had emigrated with a little company to North Africa. As a matter of fact, and as Augustine discovered upon the monk's visiting Hippo, Leporius had imbibed with his Pelagian poison a vague belief concerning the person of Christ. "It was not God Himself," he declared, "who was born as man, but a perfect man was born with God." This is a kind of hearkening forward to the confusion of Nestorius. In Carthage, Augustine achieved the distinction of winning this Gallic monk back to the faith, and leading him to a public recantation of his error.

In all this, it will be seen how Augustine devoted himself until the end to the work of purging the Church of error. Even when the Vandal hordes were pressing towards Hippo, and pounding at the city gates, he was conscientiously toiling at the longest of all his works, the vast anti-Pelagian project elicited by the treatises of Julian of Eclanum. As already noted, this zeal for Catholic opinion brought him into conflict with the growing pretensions of Rome. No sooner was the first controversy with Zosimus over, than Augustine was drawn into another, not so far-reaching in its direct results, but bringing to a climax the North African revolt from the domination of the Roman bishopric.

A short time before, Bishop Urbanus, of Sicca, a former pupil of Augustine, had condemned and dismissed one of his priests, Apiarius by name, for reprehensible conduct. Appeal was at once made to Rome. Zosimus, ready to grasp at anything which meant to him an increase of prestige, sustained the appeal. A legate was sent in haste to demand the reinstatement of Apiarius. Faustinus, an arrogant Italian bishop, who bore the message, cited two canons of Nicæa in support of the claim of Zosimus that Rome had a right to interfere and be obeyed. As a matter of history, these particular canons were not added till later. Great was the astonishment of Aurelius and his fellow-bishops, therefore, when they found the decrees absent from their authentic copies of the doings of the Nicene Council. However, they were willing to admit them, pending an investigation. But their liberty and manhood were nevertheless at stake, and they gave expression to their concern by ordaining that, whoever, thereafter, instead of appealing to the jurisdiction of the North African Church, appealed to one beyond the sea, should be excluded from the fellowship of the Church. This was in keeping with a spirit of ecclesiastical freedom which had manifested itself in North Africa from the earliest times.[2]

How Zosimus would have treated the question of Rome's supremacy, had he lived, we can not tell. His death, in December of 418, left the question to the settlement of other minds. His immediate successor, Boniface, reappointed the despised Faustinus, who, at a council of African bishops, held in Carthage late in May of the following year, impatiently renewed his haughty assertions about the pretended canons. It was finally agreed to regard them as legitimate, but to send to the bishops of Alexandria, Constantinople, and Antioch, for confirmation.

Although Augustine maintains a tantalizing silence on the subject, we can not doubt that the reply soon received from the distant Churches must have exasperated him greatly. For all three bishops forwarded authentic copies of the Nicene canons, and, lo! there was no trace of the articles so stoutly proclaimed by Zosimus, and defended by his legate. This was not the end of the matter, however. Although he had been restored, the base character of Apiarius could not long remain hidden. In a few years, he suffered a second dismissal

---

[2] See Neander, II, p. 174 f.

for unmanly conduct, and a second time appealed to Rome. Cælestine, whom Augustine addresses in most affectionate terms in Epistle 192, had succeeded Boniface as Bishop of Rome in 423. But any friendship he had for Augustine was outweighed by his zeal for the exaltation of Rome. He welcomed Apiarius, and once more selected the obnoxious Faustinus to represent him before the African bishops. With them, however, the case was prejudged. Faustinus encountered a violent opposition. It is difficult to imagine the outcome, had not Apiarius acknowledged his guilt, and thereby silenced the "pompousness" of Rome. At any rate the bishops directed to Cælestine a letter which was a veritable declaration of independence. Throughout is manifest the vigor of Augustine, who signed the document.

Shortly after these events, on the other hand, Augustine had, to say the least, paid a rather remarkable tribute of respect to the bishop of Rome, in the form of a request for his advice, in a tangle which was greatly disturbing the bishop of Hippo.[3] Not far from the district of Hippo was a small town named Fussala. Formally the Donatists had completely dominated the surrounding country, and not one Catholic was to be found in the town. By great sacrifice, even of life, a little communion had been established there, and under Augustine's direction a chapel was erected. Then, as it was impossible

---

[3] See Ep. 209, entire. The letter is sometimes called in question.

to keep the growing work under his eye, Augustine made a separate parish of it, and proceeded thither for the ordination of a bishop. For that purpose he invited from a distance the aged primate of Numidia. Great was his chagrin, at the last moment, to find his candidate for the office of bishop unwilling to serve. It was seemingly out of the question to postpone the ordination, though Augustine admits in his letter to Cælestine that it would have been more prudent. Among his companions was a young man named Antonius, who had been reared "from childhood" in his monastery, but, withal, a lad of no experience, except as a "reader." Augustine confesses with confusion that it was a great risk to take, and overhasty, but Antonius was made bishop on the spot.

This was in 418. By 422, the Fussalenses had had enough of their youthful bishop. Charges of intolerable tyranny and spoilation, of extortion, covetousness, and oppression, were preferred against him, and Augustine was asked to remove him. Instead, a council was called and Antonius, though found guilty on minor counts, was allowed to retain his office with restricted powers. The whole affair came to the ears of Boniface through Antonius himself, who complained that he had been abused. Boniface, flattered by the appeal to himself, demanded, with a threat of violence, the full reinstatement of Antonius. The Roman bishop's death at this juncture left the disturbance in the hands of Cælestine. It was being rumored that imperial power was about to be used to restore Antonius, and heavy criticism was directed against Augustine. This led to the letter already mentioned. Augustine, without malice towards the Fussalenses, and with an evident desire for fairness all around, urges Cælestine to show compassion. Indeed, he even declares that anxiety over this unfortunate business had all but driven him to retirement from his episcopal office. The following year came the break with Rome, and we hear nothing more of the case.

As belonging among the events of this closing period, mention is generally made of certain miracles which are said to have been performed at Hippo about the year 424. These Augustine details at great length, and with simple faith, in the last book of "The City of God." Some years previous, so it was declared, certain bones of the martyr Stephen had been brought from the Holy Land to Africa. Wherever they were carried, according to the testimony of men like Possidius and Evodius, strange and wonderful deeds were wrought. At Hippo, Augustine received a portion of the relics with great joy, and had them enshrined in a chapel by themselves. Two years after, he announces himself as bewildered by the large number of miraculous occurrences, to which he bears unquestioning witness. "Were I to be silent of all others, and to record exclusively the miracles of healing which were wrought in Calama and Hippo by means of this martyr, *they would fill volumes."* Of those actually published, he knows of seventy, but the unpublished ones were "incomparably more."[4]

For the most part, these miracles had to do with devil-possession. There are some more fantastic. Several were cases of the raising of the dead. Augustine seems to have been at pains to get full evidence in each case. But his investigations would not pass muster to-day. In the episode of the Syrian, Bassus, for example, there is surprisingly slim proof of all the facts. This man's daughter was perilously ill, and he had brought her dress to the shrine of Stephen. Upon returning home, "his servants ran from the house to tell him she was dead." He found the household in tears. Throwing upon "his daughter's body the dress he was carrying, she was restored to life." Augustine speaks of "the martyr himself, by whose prayers she was healed"—a species of superstition for which there is no authority whatever in the Christianity of the early Church.

No doubt the most exciting of these "miracles" was the reputed healing of Paulus and Palladia, a brother and sister from the Cappadocian Cæsarea. Together with six other brothers and two sisters, they had been cursed by their mother for some wrong they had done her (Augustine inserts no disapproval), and were all "seized with a hideous

---

[4] City of God, Bk. XXII, Ch. VIII.

shaking in all their limbs." The credulity of Augustine in this instance is remarkably naïve. Reluctantly one is forced to believe that it was only the eagerness for an unanswerable defense of his faith, that led him in old age to such artless acceptance of easily explained, even if unusual, occurrences.

Even more spectacular, but with similar results, was the cure of Palladia. It is regrettable that so masterful a mind as Augustine's did not break away from the superstitions of that decadent age and blaze a new path for himself and for the mediæval Church.

The labors of Augustine at this time were not only abundant for a man of ripe years; they were becoming oppressive. He had requested his people to leave him in quiet, but they had continued to throng him as before. He was unwilling, moreover, to leave the choice of his successor till after his death; for experience had taught him that dissension often accompanied these elections. It was contrary to his policy to think of choosing a coadjutor, following the precedent set in his own case. Accordingly, he decided to have the people appoint a successor-designate, to whom could be intrusted most of the responsibilities of office. We have a most readable record, prepared by Augustine himself, of the proceedings which followed.[5]

There is little basis left us for a fair estimate of

---

[5] See Ep. 213.

the new bishop-elect. Augustine was satisfied, and his people certainly had no question to raise. For only four years was Bishop Eraclius to stand at the older man's side, and then, with the tragic termination of the work in Hippo, he was to be without further opportunity to give his particular talent full play.

Indeed, North Africa and its Churches was already doomed. And it was a part of the bitter experiences of Augustine's last year of life that one of his trusted admirers was so intimately involved in the inevitable ruin. For twenty-five years, the empire was ruled by a woman, Placidia, mother of the Emperor Valentinian III. She had placed the province of Africa in the hands of a noble Christian general, the Count Boniface. With him Augustine began to have pleasant relations as early as 418. Within a year or two his wife died, and the sorrowing count was nearly persuaded to enter a monastery. At this crisis, Augustine showed that the charge of his being unpractical, sometimes made against him, is groundless. He induced Boniface to remain at his important post, though adding, after the manner of his time, the advice that he should not remarry. To this program Boniface agreed. But, alas! for human weakness. He was soon ensnared by the wiles of a Vandal princess in Spain, and married her. Augustine sought to find comfort in the fact that Pelagia turned Catholic with her marriage. But his comfort could hardly have been deep when rumors came to his ears that the count was not proving true to his new wife. At any rate, he watched the subsequent events in the life of Boniface with increasing regret.

In the court of Placidia, few had so much influence as Ætius. He was shrewd and ambitious. In the way of his schemes stood Boniface, and he hastened straightway to effect a plan for the African count's downfall. First, Placidia was persuaded that Boniface had formed a selfish alliance with the king of the Vandals, through the marriage with Pelagia. Thus Ætius succeeded in accomplishing the recall of his rival. Simultaneously, he wrote to Boniface urging him not to obey, since his return from Africa would mean political ruin and probably death. Acting upon this advice, Boniface refused to heed the imperial mandate. The royal mother naturally looked upon such open rebellion as a proof of the pretended suspicions of Ætius. Three armies were sent against Boniface, and he defeated them all. But he knew too well his comparative weakness, and the certainty of his ultimate overthrow. In his desperation, and all unheeding the treachery of the unscrupulous Ætius, he sent to Gonderic, king of the Vandals in Spain, an offer of alliance. It was agreed at length that Boniface should yield control of two-thirds of the provinces to his new allies. Genseric, brother of Gonderic, and after the latter's death his successor, made immediate preparations for the expedition. In Spain his people were without a rival since the expulsion of the Visigoths. But Africa offered a field for even wider empire. With an unwieldy army of over fifty thousand men, Genseric set sail across the strait to Africa, early in 429.

Until Boniface was deep in the meshes of his fatal alliance, Augustine found no opportunity of addressing him. Everything was uncertain, and messengers were not to be relied upon. But the letter which finally reached the count, from the feeble bishop, proved that Augustine's mental power and great courage were not failing, as he beheld old age and grave dangers approaching. There is no mincing of words and no fruitless flattery in the letter. It is the wise, sympathetic, anxious word of a father counseling his erring son. Augustine appears ignorant of the fraud of which his distinguished friend was the victim, and for that reason rather misjudges his motives. But even so, he can not quite reconcile the earlier zeal by which Boniface tended to perpetuate the Church in Africa, through imperial protection, with his present selfishness in allowing the Vandals to lay waste the entire province. It was not "secular counsel" which the count needed. Therefore Augustine frankly avows he has none to give. He turns to the more difficult task of counseling him "in reference to God," understanding well how slow friends are to offer such advice. There is sympathetic recognition of the embarrassments into which the unfortunate man has fallen. But Augustine dares to suggest that, had it not been for Boniface's "love of the good things of the world," he would not now be in such peril. In short, he can offer but one way of escape: let him renounce his whole present position. "Show you are a brave man. Vanquish the desires with which the world is loved. Do penance for the evils of your past life. Give alms, pour forth prayers, practice fasting." Here was a dignified, uncompromising call to duty. Augustine saw that the one hope for Boniface, whatever became of Africa, was to rise to the moral height of the Christian demands upon him. Besides such considerations, "secular counsel" (the absence of which, in the letter, is so bitterly lamented by writers like McCabe), was of no importance.[6]

Looking at it merely from the secular side, we may say that Count Boniface fortunately was spared the necessity of doing anything so heroic. At any rate, he was freed from the embarrassment of being at enmity with the ruling powers. Placidia sent a trusted ambassador, Count Darius (whose favor and friendship Augustine was delighted to win, though they did not meet[7]), to seek peace with Boniface. The plot of Ætius was quickly laid bare, and the Count of Africa returned to his former allegiance. But it was then too late to close the flood gate. The restless, blue-eyed, covetous barbarians were not to be swept back.

---

[6] See Ep. 220.   [7] See Eps. 229-231.

The Final Struggle. 237

The Vandals were in the hands of a far-seeing, fearless leader. For fifty years after these events, Genseric continued to push his conquests in all directions. He ruled the Mediterranean, and swept down upon Rome with torch and sword. If Attila was "the scourge of God," Genseric was His lightning. He was both dreadful and cunning. He held back neither from cruelty nor treachery, if he might satisfy his all-consuming avarice. With his following of wild Vandals and nomad Moors, he had already devastated a large area of Mauritania. "Soon they reached the broad roads that the Romans had constructed along the coast and the outlying towns. They poured themselves over the fields and orchards, leaving only a waste of blackened stubble and uprooted trees behind them. They swept down upon the cities with a bitter scorn for their civilization or their Trinitarian religion, and an insatiable thirst for gold." The student of Gibbon will recall how these rapacious Arians made cruel use of their difference of faith to demolish Christian churches and subject the members and priests to horrible, inhuman treatment.

But now Boniface was ready to restore the provinces to peace and order. He sent word to Genseric that there was no further need for him in Africa, and he might lead his plunderers back to his empire in Spain. But the rich plains of Numidia were just in sight, and the Vandal king had measured his strength. His back was turned to a desolate country, and he faced a land of promise whose people were disorganized. A brief truce was declared, during which Genseric haughtily spurned the proposition of Boniface to buy him off. He saw farther than a paltry ransom. And, as his only barrier to success was the army of the count of Africa, it was necessary for them to cross swords at once. A bloody battle ensued, in which Boniface exhausted his skill in a final effort in behalf of the empire. The fury of Genseric could not be stayed. Forcing his enemy into the walled city of Hippo, he sat down before its gates to await his day.

What was the state of mind of the bishop of Hippo on that memorable day of May, 430, when the siege was begun, can be only conjectured. Certainly he could expect nothing but defeat, however long delayed. Hippo occupied a strong defensive position. But help must come mostly from within. The empire was held too loosely together for Rome to hear and heed the cry for help. Moreover, the ruin of Numidia, and of the bishopric of Hippo, meant to Augustine the ruin of all his life-work. It was a sad picture that met his eyes, as he stood upon the central hill of the city, and beheld the surrounding province wreathed in lurid lines of smoke. Strange indeed was the contrast between all this tumbling into oblivion of his prodigious efforts, and the inner consciousness that North Africa was now his and the Church's. The old enemies of the Catholic doctrine were in full retreat. Paganism was being forgotten as a relic. The Militant Church of Christ was dominant everywhere. But now, conflagration and waste met his anxious gaze on every hand. And the Arian Vandal held the entire city in a tightening grip.

But Augustine was not dismayed. His calm faith in God led him to look upon the situation without a tremor. Each day, as long as the waning strength of his seventy-six years would allow, he preached to the wondering populace, inspiring them with fresh courage.

Thus the siege wore on for many a weary month. Early in August a fever laid hold of the venerable bishop, and he was forced to remain in his room. Possidius relates how, on his bed of sickness, a sick man was brought to him, and Augustine was besought to cure him. At first he refused. If he were able to work miracles, he said jocosely, he would heal himself. But they urged him till he stretched forth his hands, and the man was wondrously cured. This is the only miracle with which Augustine is credited. A fortnight before his death he bade his friends farewell, and ordered that he be left alone in his own room, except for the necessary visits of his physician and attendants. Written large on the walls beside him were the psalms of penitence. On the twenty-eighth of August, 430, the end came. He died in full possession of his faculties and in full peace. Thus, amid the tumults of the City of Men his soul passed on to the long-cherished sight of the holy City of God. "He made no will," says Possidius (who was with Augustine until the last), "since he was one of God's paupers and had nothing from which to make one. His library he ordered should be given to his Church, and all his writings, forever guarded by posterity."

Nearly a year passed after the death of Augustine, and Hippo was still intact. In the fourteenth month, Genseric was obliged to raise the siege, and the inhabitants escaped, by sea, to Italy. But the city was lost to the empire, through a second defeat of Boniface, while the Vandals poured through the gates to plunder and burn. The precious books of Augustine, the record goes, and his church, were preserved amid the general disaster. Two centuries later, the Arabs completed the ruin of the former city, leaving to coming centuries a dust-heap and an imperishable memory.

Darkness closes over these outward remains of the work of Augustine, but not over his name. Admitting the presence in him of divers deplorable defects, we are far from grudging a tribute to the commanding genius of a man who stands out in marked contrast to the dark, unstable age in which he lived, and has shed an influence for good over all succeeding ages. Augustine saw past the fading glories of this world, and riveted the attention of men upon the things of enduring value. He was exemplary also as a loyal Catholic. We can not impeach the zeal and self-repressive devotion with which he gave himself to the aggrandizement of the Church. He has made the world see her majesty—in the words of Reuter, "the grandeur of her organization, the ordered ranks of her episcopate, the authority of her tradition, the rich resources of her means of grace." His "theology of grace" has, at least, had the credit of lifting up the indispensable, absolutely essential preparatory work which God has done for our salvation. He has enriched literature and human life by all he contributed of mind and heart. It is not saying too much, to declare that he was as necessary to his age as was Paul to his, or Luther and Cromwell and Lincoln to theirs. It was God who gave them all, each one to his own time.

CHAPTER XVI.

THE STREAM OF AUGUSTINIANISM.

One is not to suppose that Augustine's identity with his own age shuts him off from a masterful influence upon succeeding generations. It is not merely that he turned out to be the schoolmaster of the Middle Ages. There is a silent pressure of his power felt in every period of the history of the Church and of Christian doctrine. Indeed, it is but very recently that admission has been made of the decadence of his teaching. Although the Augustinian view of things has held sway for nearly a millennium and a half, writes one critic, to-day his "empire over religious thought is trembling."[1] Another makes complaint of the "lingering hold of Augustine upon the modern mind." He judges that "the tenets of the Bishop of Hippo have been for so many years identified with divine revelation, that it requires an intellectual revolution in order to attain the freedom to interpret correctly, not only the early Fathers of the Church, but Scripture itself."[2] This is undoubtedly true. But it must not be overlooked

---

[1] Brierly, The Eternal Religion, p. 36.
[2] Allen, Continuity of Christian Thought, p. 11. Cf. also the remarkable charge made on page 170.

that the necessary "intellectual revolution" has already taken place.

With almost equal enthusiasm, and of course for very opposite reasons, Augustine has been esteemed by both Protestants and Romanists. His canonization by the latter was most fitting, and has long since ceased to excite wonder. Perhaps it is an exaggeration to say he was the Father of Roman Catholicism. Justice requires a moderation of that oft-repeated statement. Certainly he never would have given conscious consent to the later extraordinary developments of his conceptions of the Church. But it must be conceded that Catholicism had its roots in Augustine, and it is not inconceivable that the growth was a natural one.[3]

Extended reference has previously been made to Augustine's doctrine of the Church. He regarded the Church as a thoroughly equipped, omnipotent society, whose organization, institutions, and heaven-given rights were not to be called in question. Of the necessity for a supreme organ of infallible authority, such as later became centralized in Rome, he had not even a remote idea. But there were elements in him, such as his insistence upon the universality and exclusiveness of the Church, his doctrine of baptism, and his intolerant treatment

---

[3] Cf. Robertson, in Regnum Dei: "He registers for us the beginning of a process the full nature of which he could not fully realize; a process which could only be embodied, in fact, in conditions which Augustine neither knew nor foresaw, but which were none the less, even then, on their way to fulfillment."

of heretics, which made possible the papacy. He appropriated the saying of Cyprian: "Outside the Church salvation is impossible." And he added: "I would not believe the Gospel except the authority of the Catholic Church had moved me."

The immediate results of such extreme ideas are difficult to trace. Scarcely a decade had passed after Augustine's death, before Leo the Great demanded supremacy for the authority of Rome, thus establishing the papacy upon a claim which has never been yielded. A century and a half later, Pope Gregory I, building upon Augustinian foundations, made salvation dependent upon meritorious works, and purgatory a necessity. This type of teaching—"a sacred tradition, attested by ecclesiastical authority, the validity of which it was impious to doubt"—was passed on to the Middle Ages by the influences of hierarchical prerogative. Scholasticism, proclaiming the infallibility and superior rights of the pope, followed hard upon. Its renowned champion, Thomas Aquinas, was in many respects an echo of Augustine, so that the saying goes, "There is but one path to Augustine; it is by way of Aquinas." The most striking modern phase of this stream of tendency was the Tractarian Movement, with John Henry Newman as its leading spirit. On him the marks of Augustine are pronounced.[4]

---

[4] Cf. Fisher: "Newman's memory was haunted by the sounding phrase of Augustine, 'Securus judicat orbis terrarum.'" History of Christian Doctrine, p. 459.

We must conclude, therefore, that in Augustine were the germs of the mighty Roman Church. He was the defender of Catholic authority, and the apostle of ecclesiastical imperialism. In this, that part of the Church which acknowledges the sole authority of a Divine Person, speaking through an unfettered conscience, can not follow him. There is, however, something to be said in Augustine's favor. He could not have foreseen the inevitable outworkings of his own theories. Moreover, as we have seen, there was a special appropriateness to that age in the idea of a high ecclesiastical authority. In the presence of the oversweeping forces of a crude barbarism the majestic power of an organized Church was simply "a providential adaptation of Christianity to a lower environment." According to Guizot, it was only such a Church that could defend itself against the barbarians and the internal decay of the empire.

On the other hand, Augustine has made a deep impress upon certain ideas classed as essentially Protestant. Dissent from the principle of predestination early asserted itself in Hilary of Arles, and in John Cassian. Still later (about 850), when the monk Gottschalk announced a rigid Augustinian doctrine of election, he was condemned, scourged, and imprisoned for life. But the pronounced predestinarian notion was only slumbering. Luther— together with Wiclif and Huss—was a profound student of Augustine, whom he considered the mightiest of the Fathers. And he revived the characteristic teaching about election in all its rigor; every separate sin, in his view, is determined by the sovereign will of God. Space will not permit of a close pursuit of this stream of thought. Augustine begot Calvin. Jansenism, the Thirty-nine Articles, the Westminster Confession, the Federal theology of the seventeenth century, the later writings of Edwards and Mozley and the Princeton theologians, the sermons of Spurgeon, and the latest contentions of Professor Orr,—all bear witness to the virility of the predestinarianism so stoutly asserted by Augustine.

Happily and hopefully, the Protestant world is refusing more and more to accept the repugnant deterministic elements of Augustine's theology. "A reduction of the area of Calvinism" is admitted by so eminent an authority as Professor Fisher.[5] An even more recent writer speaks of "the almost universal abandonment of that merciless logic which reads in the will of God the denial of the human will, and the absolute, irrevocable doom before their birth of a majority of the human race."[6] At all

---

[5] History of Christian Doctrine, p. 549.

[6] Professor C. T. Winchester, The Life of John Wesley, p. 209. In this exceedingly able book, Professor Winchester's remark (p. 105) that "the evangelist, though he may think like a Calvinist in his study, must preach like an Arminian in the fields and the streets," reminds one of Richard Garnet's *mot* about the mother of Carlyle: "As a Calvinist she is certain that Tom's fate is fixed from eternity, and as a mother is equally sure that he may go to heaven if he will." Certainly an *evangelist ought* to be able to preach anywhere what he believes, and vice versa.

events, there are few nowadays who would acquiesc in the quaint judgment of Cotton Mather, expressed in the *Magnalia:* "During the first seventy-five years of New England there had flourished so many regenerate souls that one might almost statistically infer that New England was specially favored of God." Even in Scotland, I am persuaded that Professor Denney's commentary on the Westminster Confession would be considered too hard and narrow; for he says: "Calvinism is strong because, when necessity and chance are offered to it as the alternative explanations of the universe, and even of man's destiny, it elects for necessity."[7] Dr. Stalker insists that "God is calling all, and that Christ is offered to all without distinction."[8] And Professor George Adam Smith eloquently pleads in behalf of a love in God "which dares and ventures all with the worst, with the most hopeless of us."[9] The modern mind in this matter is mirrored in the noble message of "In Memoriam:"

> " Our wills are ours, we know not how;
> Our wills are ours, to make them Thine."

With this the earlier judgment of Augustine himself was in perfect accord. "God does everything to save us," he declares, "except deprive us of our free will."

---

[7] Gospel Questions and Answers.
[8] John Knox: His Ideas and Ideals, p. 165.
[9] The Book of Isaiah, xl-lxvi.

Most of all, Augustine's tenets regarding sin and grace have found a place in the Christian thought of the centuries. It is unnecessary to revert to the perverted and undiscriminating notions of original sin. Every student of doctrine is familiar with the reappearance of those ideas in Anselm, Peter Lombard, and Aquinas. Melanchthon, with the other Lutheran Reformers, surpassed even the schoolmen in his clouding of the question of personal responsibility for personal sin. "By reason of our native corruption," he writes, "we are born guilty; and if any one chooses to add that men are guilty, also, for the fall of Adam, I make no protest." Such abhorrent ideas as these were transmitted to the present generation by the Westminster Confession, Jonathan Edwards, Professor Charles Hodge, and kindred influences. But it must be believed that a growing clearness of thought will result in a universal abandonment of Augustinian confusions on this subject. Racial corruption and a relentless law of heredity must be admitted. But, as some one has remarked, a man's accountability is not for the disposition with which he was born, but for the disposition with which he dies.

Augustine's great service was in his stern and unyielding reprobation of all that is sin. He was not the man to adopt the calm optimism of a Whitman: "There is no evil; or, if there is, I say it is just as important to you, to the land, or to me, as anything else." Nor would he assume the arrogance of another modern spirit, who unctuously proclaims that "the superior man" has ceased to be troubled about his sins. One reason why the "Confessions" continue to be read is, that they brand sin with its right name, and make no attempt to hide the worst that is true of human life. In its pages many a college boy has seen a portrait of himself, and been led thereby to a repentance that is not unto death.

It was this settled conviction of the tragedy of sin, coupled with an experimental appreciation of the meaning of grace, that has made the piety of Augustine, both in its depth and in its ardor, a type. It was reproduced in Bernard of Clairvaux, and in Richard Baxter. Its fundamental position, that "whatsoever is without God is not sweet," gives us an impressive insight into the more spiritual side of the doctrine of sovereign will. Had Augustine's thought of God ended with devotional yearnings and aspirations, instead of breaking over into disavowal of human freedom, there would be less in him to regret.

With all his passion and piety, for which he will continue to remain a spiritual guide to thousands, I must believe that the final judgment about Augustine will be that he does not represent the highest (the New Testament) view of Christianity. He had glimpses of it. Sometimes he touches profoundly some of the vital things. But the sweeping, organic thought of Christianity did not seize upon him. There is in him no central place for the illuminating, all-determining person and work of our Lord. And he dwells little upon the unflagging ministry of the Holy Spirit. It is equally true that Augustine fails in estimating human nature. He never grasped the meaning of personality. Mitigations and explanations there may be, and are, a plenty. But we are not to permit the glamour of his own story, told with such spiritual fascination, or the passionate piety with which he acknowledged his debt to the Church and to the "irresistible" grace of God, to win us to an unqualified approval of all his doctrinal conclusions as if they were inerrant.

www.ingramcontent.com/pod-product-compliance
Lightning Source LLC
Chambersburg PA
CBHW070247230426
43664CB00014B/2429